Foreign Brides From Antiquity

by

Frank and Elizabeth Haines

Published by Hobby House Press, Cumberland, Maryland 21502

Table of Contents

ISBN: 0-87588-346-X

Introduction

When we began this program, we had no idea of its scope or where it would lead us but it tells us not only of wedding customs and costumes, but also the status of women throughout history. Our brides have interesting stories to tell.

Since marriage is considered to be a holy estate, it seems appropriate to begin with a quotation from the Book of Genesis: "And the Lord God said, 'It is not good that the man should be alone; I will make him a help meet for him.' And out of the ground the Lord God formed every beast of the field, and every fowl of the air; and brought them unto Adam to see what he would call them: and whatsoever Adam called every living creature, that was the name thereof. And Adam gave names to all cattle, and to the fowl of the air, and to every beast of the field; but for Adam there was not found a help meet for him. And the Lord God caused a deep sleep to fall upon Adam, and he slept; and he took one of his ribs, and closed up the flesh instead thereof. And the rib, which the Lord God had taken from man, made he a woman, and brought her unto the man. Therefore shall a man leave his father and his mother, and shall cleave unto his wife: and they shall be one flesh."

The first bride and groom were one flesh, for Eve was taken from Adam's side. Folklore gives us many reasons for this choice. We especially like this one from the rabbis. They claim that Eve could not be taken from the head, then she would be vain; if from the eyes, wanton; the mouth, gossip; the ears, eavesdrop; the hands, meddlesome; the feet, gadabout; and the heart, jealousy. Then some cynic, probably a man, said that these precautions were quite useless for women have all of these faults anyway!

For the comfort of our feminine egos, many other legends take an equally uncomplimentary view of Adam, maintaining that originally he was like a beast — coarse, rude and inarticulate — and that Eve gave him his upright position, polish and spirituality.

With use, Eve's name became synonymous with that of woman. However, in ancient Hebrew it means "Mother of All Living."

So we salute Eve, the first bride, but she is not represented here because a fig leaf did not offer much of a costuming challenge. Before introducing our brides, we will note that it is believed that all mating was promiscuous; then tribal law established that all wives belonged to all men; then the desire for a single wife led to marriage by capture. Man began stealing brides from other tribes and as this was dangerous, he frequently asked his best friend to accompany him, so now we have our "best man." To avoid tribal wars, men next bought their brides, introducing marriage by purchase. They now paid for the privilege of having one wife; the bride-price also reimbursed her parents for the loss of their daughter and her services.

Marriage as a religious contract was observed by some pagans and a few early Christians; however, the records of ancient civilizations show that for centuries marriage was basically a business agreement, later legalized by civil contract.

BIBIYAH

Babylon, 1600 B.C.

For our first bride we go to Babylon, 1600 B.C. Her name is Bibiyah. We took it from a Babylonian love letter of the time: "To Bibiyah. May the God Shamas and the God Marduk forever endow you with good health. I sent a messenger to inquire of your whereabouts. Please tell me how you are. I have come to Babylon and saw you not. Ah, I am so sad."

Bibiyah is a composite figure for she represents an early form of that country's wedding custom, Pagan Group Marriage, as well as the later Civil Marriage established by King Hammurabi, the great Babylonian lawgiver.

Costume

Her costume is also composite. She wears the wedding ring of the early form and the costume of a court lady of Hammurabi's time.

The Babylonians were a short, stocky people with wiry, wavy black hair. They wore wool, cotton or linen fabrics, depending on the season, and used fringes and handsome silk embroidery to decorate their garments. Bibiyah's long-sleeved heavy white linen gown is trimmed with embroidered bands, with a plain linen beneath, except for a narrow embroidery at the neck. The brilliant embroidery shows a typical geometric design.

Sandals or rough leather slippers were sometimes worn but mostly the people went barefoot.

Babylonian women were fond of makeup; blue eye shadow and heavy black accents on eyebrows and eyelashes was fashionable at this time.

Bibiyah's headdress is adapted from ones in the Cairo and University of Pennsylvania Museums. A number of such headdresses were found in various Babylonian tombs. It is not necessarily a bridal headdress, but for this important ceremony, it was customary to wear new clothes and as much jewelry as the bride owned. The lovely flower and leaf forms of the headdress with the blue lapis centers of the flowers show the Babylonians' fine sense of design and superb workmanship.

The olive-shaped clay bead with the couple's names and marriage date inscribed on it was worn around Bibiyah's neck on a cord, the equivalent of our wedding ring.

Customs

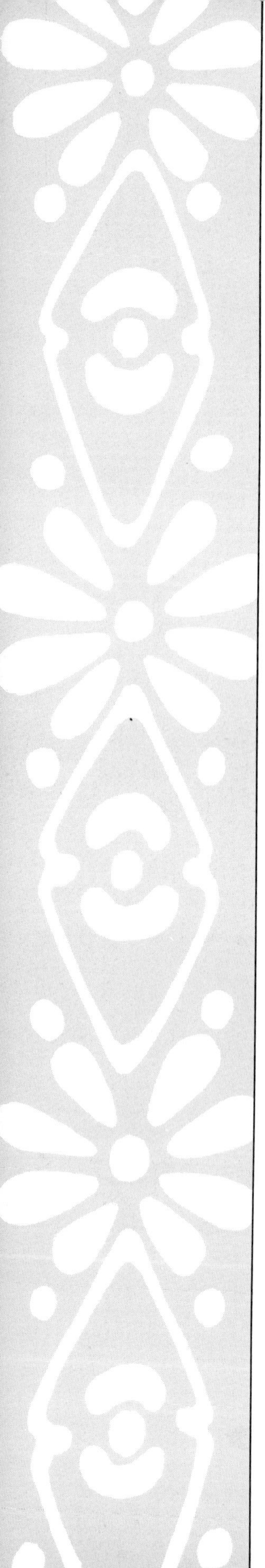

No girl in ancient Babylon ever worried about getting married for custom established an ingenious answer to providing husbands for all marriageable girls, pretty or homely, rich or poor, every girl was sure to be married before the auction was over. Once a year, in the month of Sabat (corresponding to our February), an annual marriage auction was held in the plaza before the temple. The auction was held in two parts, beginning with the most beautiful girl being offered first, and proceeding on a descending scale of feminine attractiveness. The second part of the auction began with the least desirable candidate, perhaps crippled or deformed, and proceeded on as ascending scale, with the monies paid for the first girls providing dowries for their less fortunate sisters.

No father could give his daughter in marriage to the man of his choice, nor could any bridegroom take away the girl he had chosen without paying for her and marrying her before leaving for home. It was at this ceremony that the clay bead (wedding ring) was used.

There was a long period of social evolution between this marriage form and that developed by the code of Hammurabi which made marriage "a contract to be man and wife together" and also made legal marriage settlements obligatory, protecting the position and rights of a wife and her children. No later code in either the ancient or medieval world was so considerate of women or provided for them so justly. Marriage was legal only when recorded in writing. A scribe was called in to draw up the contract and a duplicate was properly witnessed and filed with a public notary.

These marriage contracts contained many stipulations affecting the conduct of both parties and wives' rights were jealously protected.

Divorce was optional with both parties; if the man desired one and she had been a good wife, he must return her dowry and support her as well as the children, which she raised. If she had been a bad wife, he could degrade her to the position of a slave; however, she could still sue him on the grounds of cruelty. If she could not prove this, she could resort to "Trial by Water" where her fate was decided by the gods — if she sank, she was guilty; if she floated, she was innocent.

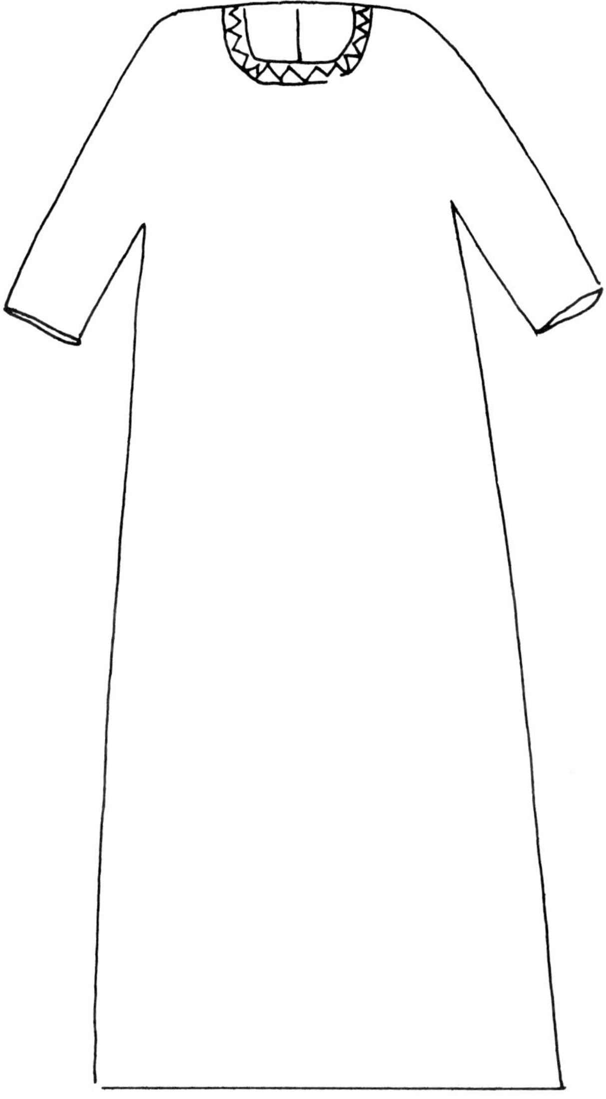

Linen under robe with embroidery at neck.

Clay bead inscribed with bridal couple's names. It was worn around the neck, the equivalent of our wedding ring.

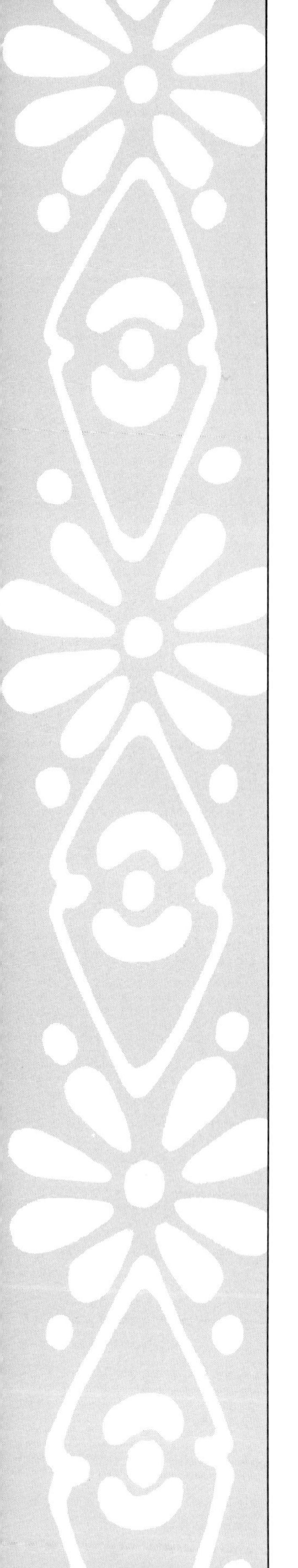

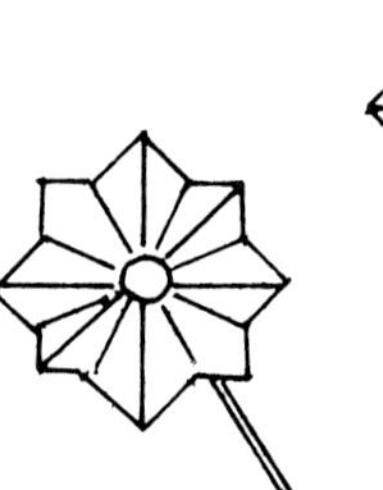

Headdress.

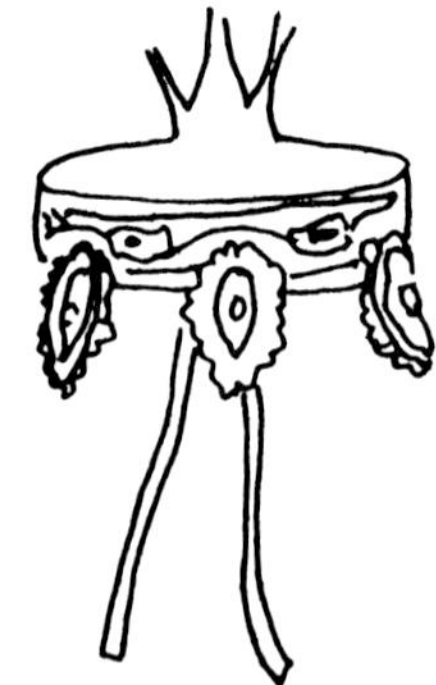

Crown holding three stars and secured by a ribbon.

Pair of gold earrings.

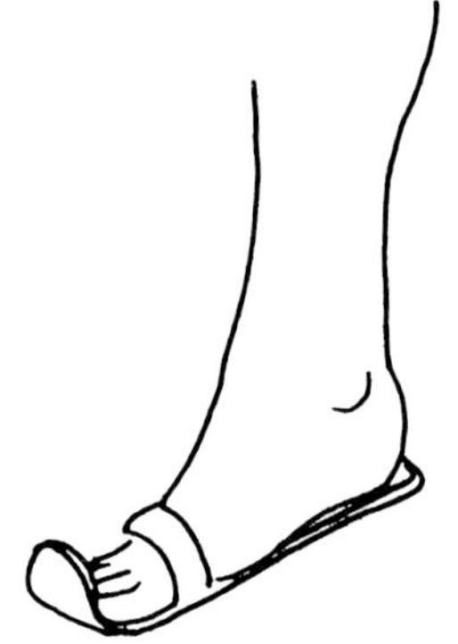

Leather sandals. No stockings.

As in all Semitic countries, the dowry was of great importance and its terms were settled at the betrothal. If a young man wished to marry a girl, his father went to her father and said, "Will you give your daughter in marriage to my son?" If the girl's father consented and if both were wealthy, generous men, they enjoyed the ensuing bargaining, coming to a settlement each knew would be acceptable from the beginning. Such a dowry might specify, "A manna of silver, three servants, a trousseau and furniture." Once this was settled, the marriage was set for a near date, provided the astrologers could agree on a lucky day.

At the wedding ceremony, the groom said to the bride, "I am the son of nobles, silver and gold shall fill thy lap, thou shalt be my wife, I will be thy husband. Like the fruit of a garden, I will give thee offspring." At the end of the ceremony the bride-price was given the bride by her father and the couple's hands were tied together with thread taken from their wedding garments, emblem of the union into which they had now entered.

The duplicate marriage contract was read before the guests and witnesses, the later signing it. The dowry and other presents were given to the groom. Prayers for the happy couple were followed by a feast with music, dancing and jesting until time to adjourn to the groom's parents' home, where the festivities continued for several days. As emblems of grace and fertility, palms were always used lavishly in the wedding decorations.

Although a girl was legally considered to be her father's property, Babylonian daughters were almost equal in importance to sons and were well educated. They were taught reading, writing, grammer and arithmetic as well as the religious myths of their race and city. They played the harp and had a knowledge of the world beyond — Egypt, Assyria and Persia. All ranks were taught to "honor thy father and thy mother" many centuries before Moses gave this as the Fifth Commandment.

A woman could be a judge, scribe, elder, secretary, witness or priestess. She could also own property in her own right, manage an estate and run a business.

In every way, their position was a high, in some ways higher, than those of 19th century English and American women — all of this in the "Land Between the Rivers" from which our civilization developed more than 4000 years ago.

QUEEN NEFERTITI

Egypt, 1375 B.C.

Queen Nefertiti represents marriage by civil contract in 1375 B.C. Her name means "beauty to come."

Of course, you recognize that this is a portrait; its famous original is in the Berlin Museum and we worked from their colored brochure and other photographs.

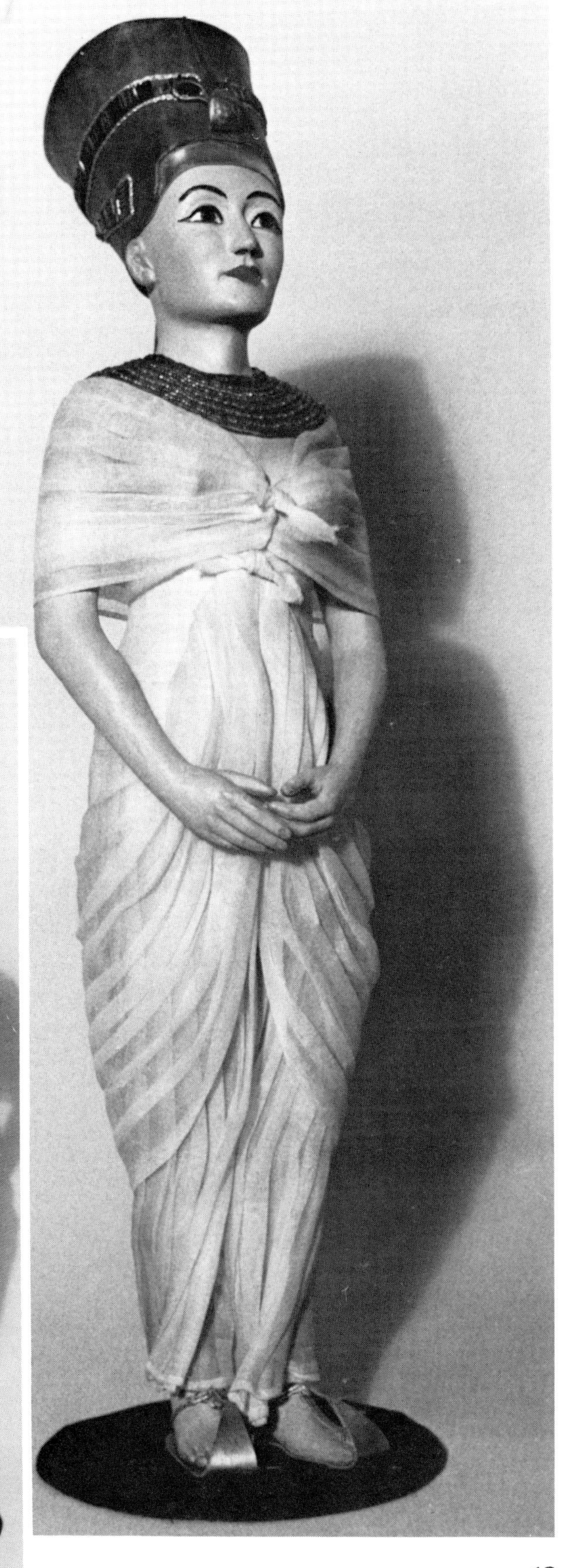

Costume

It is believed that Nefertiti's abnormally long neck was necessary to balance the weight of the crown and as there are a number of full-length drawings showing her with a normal one; that is what we used.

No Egyptian bridal dress is known but as it was customary to wear new clothes for all important occasions, we can assume that Nefertiti had something new and lovely for her wedding. The costume we show reflects the sophisticated and elegant simplicity of the court dress of the period.

Her own beautiful portrait is the most telling example of their artistic renaissance — a return to the naturalistic after years of stylization.

The leather crown, like other headdresses, was kept in a cool place until ready to be worn — a built-in cooling system. The golden asp is the symbol of royalty's power of life and death over their subjects. The green is her crown and the gold edge with the red ribbons at the back belong to her hair net, worn under the crown. Most noblewomen wore their hair "feather cut" like Nefertiti; not many at this time shaved their heads.

They loved cosmetics and perfumes as much as we do. Green eye shadow and black eyebrows and eyeliner were popular. They used lip rouge and hennaed the palms of their hands and soles of their feet; this was also considered an antiperspirant. Their nails were tinted orange.

Nefertiti's beautiful collar is characteristic of the time. Made of gold, lapis lazuli, jade and carnelian, blown glass beads and exquisite enamels were often added. Their delicate gold work was often set with turquoise for bracelets, diadems and rings. They sometimes used stylized flower motifs.

Their gowns were made of linen or the wonderfully soft long-fibered cotton. They did not have silk but their gowns were both soft and crisp, very sheer and fine. White was their favorite color and they had a passion for cleanliness. Nefertiti's's over tunic and bodice are each in one piece, with a separate skirt below, and it was that sheer. It is hot in Egypt. The "Washer" and the "Bleacher" were high court officials.

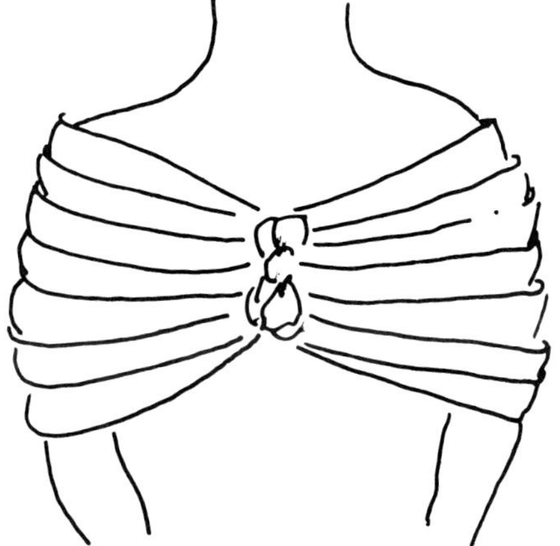

Over tunic.

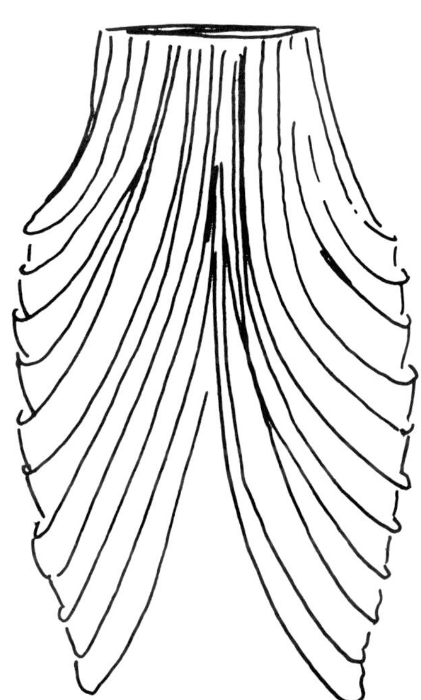

Bodice.

This bride's gold leather sandals were designed for comfort and practicality. The Egyptians had an amusing custom of putting the picture of a conquered people on their sandal soles so they were literally "treading them underfoot."

Because Egypt was, and is, dry and dusty, the care of their bodies and hair was extremely important. They bathed and oiled themselves to prevent sore eyes and cracked, painful skin. (Those little things that look like inverted flowerpots on the top of their heads in many Egyptian paintings are perfume cones, scented wax which slowly melted and ran down in fragrant, cooling streams.) No party was complete without them and each guest received a lotus flower, symbol of life and plenty.

Nefertiti represents the Egyptian ideal of beauty — short, slight, dainty, well proportioned and elegant.

She was the consort of King Ikhnaton. Together they had the courage to break tradition and become leaders in religious and governmental reform. They established a new religion, the worship of one god instead of many, endorsing simplicity in their home life and sponsoring a renaissance in the fine arts.

Previously, the pharaohs had been worshipped as gods and kept themselves remote from their subjects. Ikhnaton was the first Egyptian ruler to make himself available to his people. He took great delight being seen in public in his happy family life with Nefertiti and their six little daughters.

Although Ikhnaton's "revolution" lasted only 15 years, it had enduring effects on Egyptian life for many centuries.

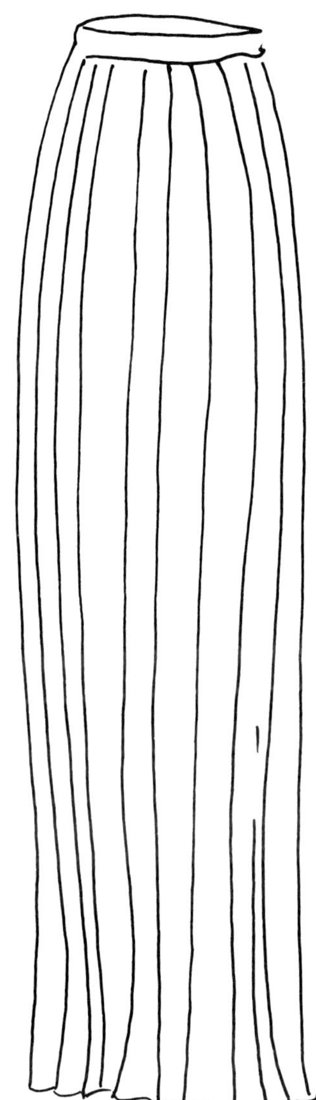

Skirt.

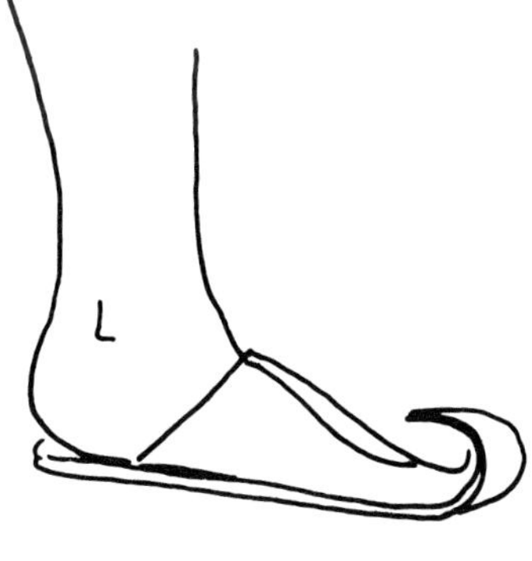

Sandals. No stockings.

Customs

To date, there are not any known records of an Egyptian marriage ceremony; however, we do know that the institution of marriage was already in use when their written records began. Now that Egypt was at the height of its glory, the women still enjoyed great privileges and freedom. The descent was through the mother's side and Nefertiti was head of the "Royal House."

In their early marriage form, the groom was absorbed into the bride's family and all property was in the wife's hands. She had full control of her husband at all times and he must make no objections to her commands, regardless of what they might be. He was regarded simply as a privileged guest in her home.

The first year of marriage was called "the year of eating," a probationary period in which either party could annul at the end by paying a specified sum of money. This early form of divorce left the principals free to remarry if this wished.

There are no records of any wedding feasts in Egyptian archaeology either, but the following description of a banquet at the home of an Egyptian gentleman could serve as an example.

The guests arrive by chariot with their servants running along beside. Those who lived nearby walked up through the gardens. They were greeted outside of the home by servants who offered them fruits and wine. Inside, rows of cakes and jars of wine were displayed on low tables. The guests sat on grass mats on the floor. Upon entering, maidens placed garlands around their necks, perfume cones on their heads and a lotus flower, symbol of plenty, in their hands.

While the royal family preferred to live simply at home, life at Court was extremely sophisticated. Elegant manners, formal table etiquette and silver knives and spoons were customary (they had no forks). For a royal service, even splash-proof silver finger bowls were provided.

All feasts began with prayers of thanksgiving and a sacrifice of fruit and wine. Entertainment was provided by music and dancing.

The feast concluded with a most curious custom — a miniature mummy in a coffin was carried among the guests. "To exhort them, while filled with wine, to make use of things present, in that all will soon be such as it is." This was just a part of their regular frame of mind.

The house would be spicy with frankincense and myrrh, for the Egyptians were accomplished perfumers.

When King Tutankhamen's tomb was opened, it was still fragrant, after 3000 years. Among its rare treasures were wreaths of natural flowers over the king's golden face mask. It is believed they were placed there by his 14-year-old widow, Nefertiti's third daughter.

The earliest known wedding contract is dated 590 B.C. We have a copy of it and will note it for you briefly. First comes the date. Then a man goes to a girl's house "to make declaration of wife" to her father, who agrees to the match and gives his daughter a dowry of "six ounces of silver and fifty measures of corn." The man swears that if he leaves her "from dislike, or preferring another" he will return the dowry plus a share of their mutual property for any children she may bear.

Woman's status was recognized by early Egyptian law. Her business position was secure if she could write and had three children. A man's first wife was his legal one and her children inherited. He took her to be his "Dear Wife" and "The Lady of His House" just as Nefertiti was "Chief Wife" and "King's Consort."

Like Nefertiti, too, wives were always represented of equal importance with their husbands in tombs for wives were considered essential to happiness in the next world.

There were many evidences that husbands were happy and followed the advice of Ptahatep, who wrote in his *Book of Wisdom*, "He who is wise, founds for himself a house, and loves his wife."

GYPTIS
Gaul, 600 B.C.

Gyptis portrays a Druid bride from ancient France, then called Gaul, 600 B.C. Many people forget that the Druids were in central France and northern Spain before they crossed the channel to the British Isles. It is believed that they originally came from India, migrating westward after some tremendous catastrophe such as a flood, earthquake, famine or epidemic.

Two unique features of their fascinating history are that at a time when other peoples had many gods, the Druids had only one, Esus. Their strange philosophy of life and death was to mourn at weddings and rejoice at funerals, for troubles begun and ended.

For centuries their priests wore gold collars and crowns and used a gold sickle to cut the sacred mistletoe. They were prophets and astrologers.

Costume

Their brides wore black and a mistletoe wreath for fertility. The Druids were excellent weavers and even at this early date were using the complicated serge weave, done on the diagonal, as Gyptis' black woolen robe shows. It is girded with bands of black wool. Her feet are bare. Her drooping head and bent shoulders were the traditional bridal pose, as though overwhelmed by the thoughts of the burdens of married life even before partaking of the wedding feast.

The bride wearing her white dress with a red and white belt and a coral necklace and bracelet.

The cup from which the bride serves the groom her first cup of wine.

Black dress tied at waist with black cord.

The bride might keep her hair in place with a black band until after the wedding.

Customs

The bride was bought from her parents, the bride-price being paid into the hollow of her father's shield. After the wedding ceremony which was performed by the High Priest under the sacred oak, the bride walked home amongst her friends. A matron walked at her left, holding before her the white shroud in which she would be buried. The priest walked at her right, chanting, in solemn rhythm, all the wifely duties awaiting her. They began, "From this day forth, young wife, thou alone wilt have to bear the burden of your united household." Omitting the archaic phrasing, it continues, "You will have to attend the baking oven, provide fuel and go in search of food; you will have to prepare the resinous torch and the lamp. You will attend the cow and even the horse if your husband requires it." Our sources do not say what the husband does but she must "Always be full of respect. You will wait upon him, standing behind him at his meals. If he chooses to take more wives, you will receive your new companions with sweetness.

"If he is angry against you and strikes you, you will pray to Esus, the only God, but you will never blame your husband, who cannot do wrong.

"If he wishes to take you with him to war, you will carry his baggage, keep his arms in good condition and nurse him if he should be sick or wounded. Happiness consists in the fulfillment of duty. Be happy, my child."

Arriving at the bride's home, she retired to a small flower-decked room where her mother or an old woman servant dyed her hair an intense red with a mixture of tallow, ashes and plaster; red hair was the sign of a married woman. Then she washed her face in beer and rubbed her neck with butter. After this, she had a light meal, then put on a white dress and collar and bracelets of bronze set with coral, or sometimes a string of red berries for decoration — red was an important symbol of life.

Her husband also wore bronze bracelets and brooches set with coral, pearls, polished pebbles or rich red enamel work. His weapons were similarly decorated.

Gyptis was now ready to receive her husband. He and his friends entered the room and she presented him with a bowl of wine, her first wifely duty.

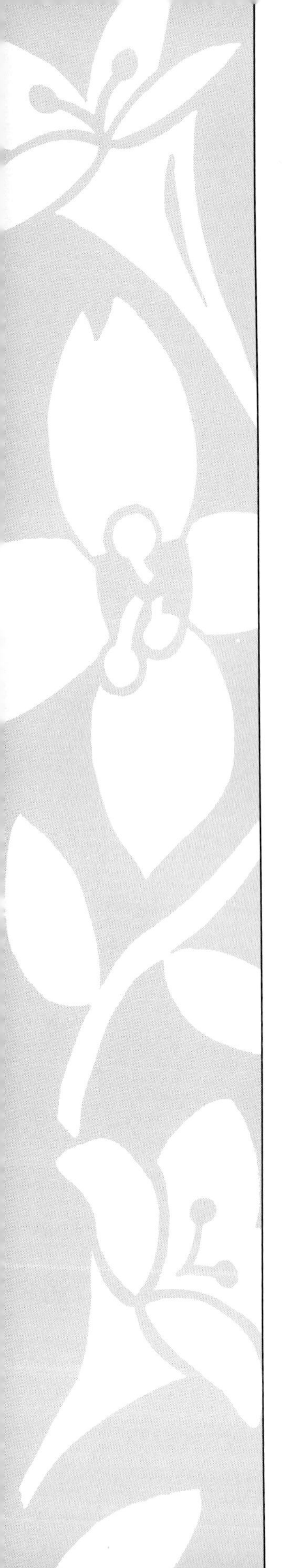

OCTAVIA

Rome, 500 B.C.

Octavia, 14 years old, represents the early Roman republic about 500 B.C. (Rome had been founded by Romulus in 753 B.C.) and they were proud that for the first 400 years there had never been a divorce. This illustrates a pagan religious ceremony.

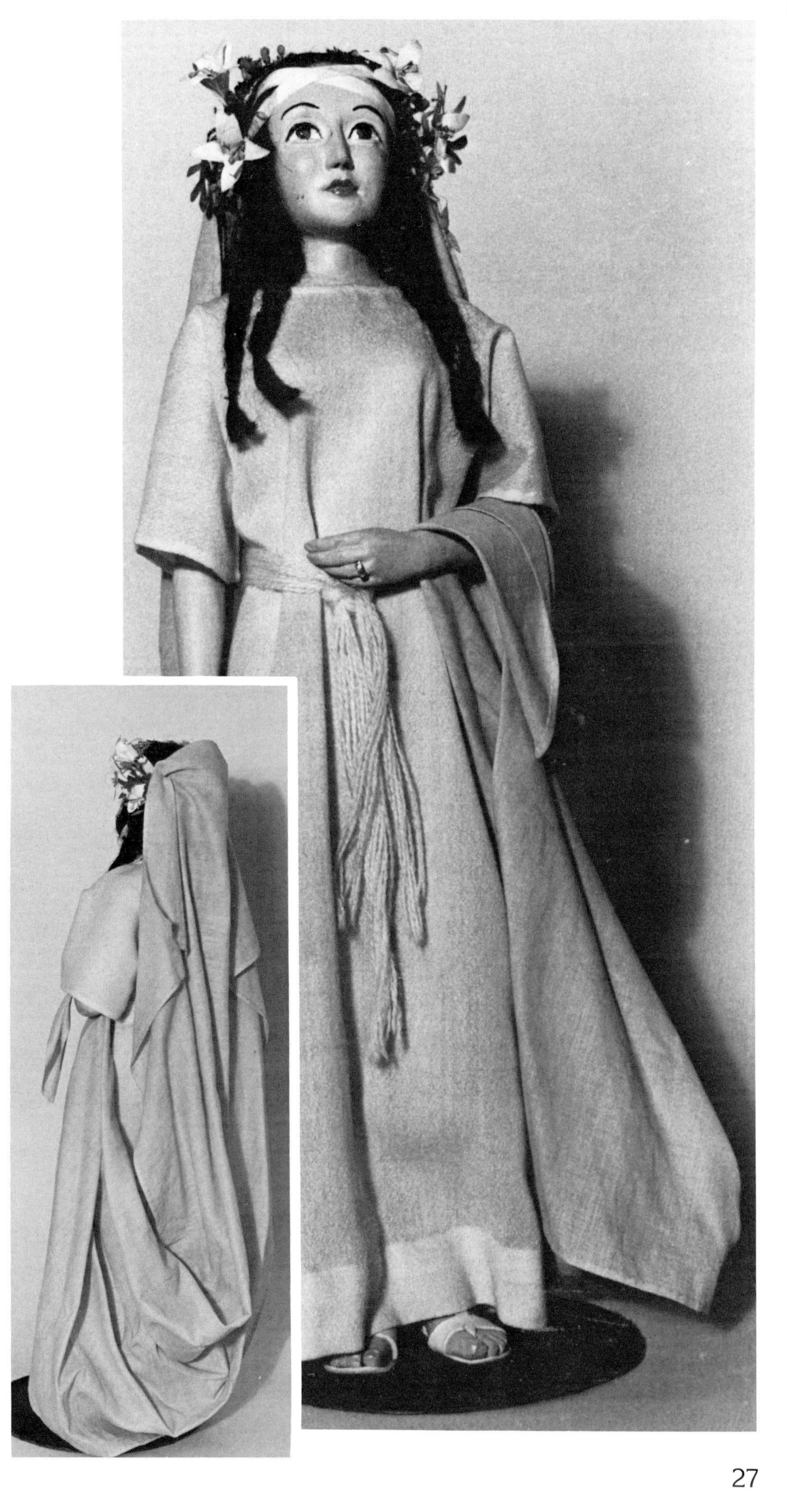

Costume

Octavia has dark eyes and hair, with the fair skin of the Romans. She wears the typical wedding gown, the tunica recta, the traditional gift from the parents to a daughter on marriage and a son on coming of age.

It was always of fine, soft cream-colored wool with a small pattern, woven on the ancient upright loom. It was in one piece, double the height of the wearer, with the selvages sewed together at the sides. The tunic was cut as little as possible, slightly under the arms and at the neckline. Its pristine condition was symbolic of the virginity of the bride.

The morning of the wedding, Octavia's mother helped her dress and secured the tunic with bands of white wool around the waist, tied in the Hercules knot, as he was the guardian of married happiness. Only the groom was then privileged to untie the knot.

Her veil was such an important part of her costume that the term "nubere," to veil oneself, was used to describe the marriage of a woman. It was the "flameum" — the flame-colored symbol of the sacred flame of Vesta, goddess of the home, giver of all life.

Octavia wears her hair in the six plaits of the early Vestal Virgins. The white ribbon securing it is arranged with crossed white ribbons in the same fashion as theirs. She would have gathered the flowers and made her garland herself the morning of the wedding — lilies for purity; wheat, fertility; rosemary, male virility; myrtle, long life and purity.

Her sandals are of soft white leather and look very much like some we wear today.

The ring was received at the time of betrothal and served as engagement and wedding ring. It was an iron signet, mark of the Roman citizen and worn, like ours, on the third finger of the left hand. The Romans also believed that the reason for this is because a vein runs directly from that finger to the heart.

The tunica recta with the Hercules knot at the waistline, tied by the mother and untied by the groom.

The iron ring, both a wedding
and an engagement ring.

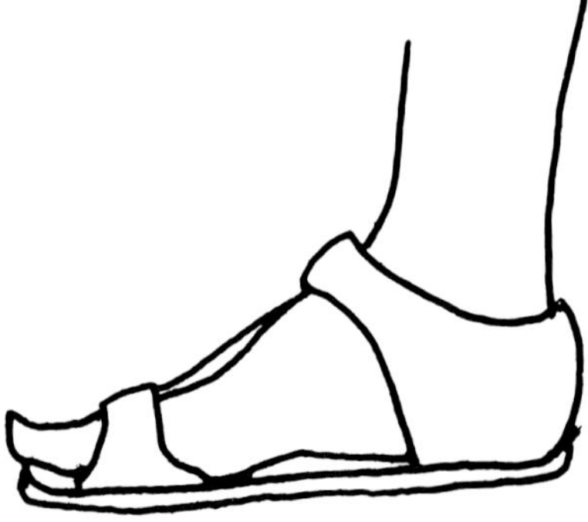

Soft white leather sandals.

Customs

Octavia's marriage would be arranged by her family and the groom's; the consent of both fathers was required.

The betrothal came first and constituted a legal bond. At this time the details of the marriage settlement were put into writing and are still used in modern civil marriages.

It was a point of honor with the Romans to provide their daughters with a dowry. If a father could not and her male relatives would not, if they had the means, a girl could compel them to do so, by law.

With the Romans, marriage was a solemn occasion, not to be entered into hastily. A groom took his bride to be a "Mater Familias," to protect his honor, bear his children and preserve and observe the family religion.

It was extremely important that the bride be acceptable to the groom's family gods as well as to his family. Each family had their own personal deities; a bride must agree to worship her husband's gods and forsake her own.

Although pagans, their vows were as sacred to them as ours are to us. They lived close to their religion in their daily life and worship.

The Romans recognized five different forms of marriage. Only one will be described here — the one most in use and requiring a religious ceremony. This was the "confarreatio" — literally, "eating of a cake together," and derived its name from "far," the old word for grain. This ceremony was believed to have the direct consent of the gods; the High Priest officiated before ten witnesses representing the families of the bridal couple. This marriage form was later restricted to priests and patricians. The ceremony was performed in three parts — the religious contract, the wedding feast and conducting the bride to her new home.

The night before the wedding, the bride dedicated her girlhood garments and golden neck ornament to her family gods. If she were 12 or under, she would dedicate her dolls and toys.

As a symbol of her virginity, she would put on the tunica recta and fine red wool hair net, like those worn at night by the Vestal Virgins.

The morning of the wedding her home would be decorated with flowers, leaves and examples of her spinning and weaving.

The ceremony was concluded at dusk when the bride was escorted to her new home. This was never omitted as it was essential to the validity of the marriage. A charming procession, led by flute players and a young boy carrying the white thorn marriage torch was viewed by everyone who waited in the street to see the bride and join in singing the marriage hymn. For this procession and the bride's arrival in her new home, we derive some more of our marriage customs.

She carried three coins, giving one to the groom as a symbol of her dowry, leaving one as a farewell gift to her family gods and the last she tossed in the street so the gods of the crossroads would permit her free passage to her new home. Some modern brides still carry lucky coins.

Upon arriving at the groom's home, he carried her over the threshold, demonstrating his right of possession and commemorating marriage by capture. At this time the bride again repeated the words of consent so all knew that she entered willingly. This put the final seal on the legality of the marriage.

Inside the house wood was laid ready for a fire. The bride kindled it with the marriage torch, after which she put it out and tossed it among the guests who scrambled for this lucky token as guests vie for the modern bride's bouquet.

The omens would have been taken when the guests arrived before sunrise. Everyone assembled in the main room and the bride and groom took their place before the family altar. The "pronuba," a respected matron, joined their hands and the bride than repeated the words of consent, "Quando to Gaius, ego Gaia." In other words, bone of my bone, and so forth. This form never varied, regardless of the names of the bridal couple.

Next, the High Priest blessed the sacred marriage cake, after which it was eaten by the bride and groom. It is believed to be a pagan form of our Christian communion.

Then came the wedding feast, which concluded with a different wedding cake being served to the guests. This was the "mustaceum," and like the marriage cake, derived its name from an ingredient — "must," unfermented grape juice.

There are several recipes for these wedding cakes. The following is Cato's. "Sprinkle a peck of flour with must, add anise,

Bibiyah —
Babylon, 1600 B.C.

Queen Nefertiti —
Egypt, 1375 B.C.

Gyptis —
Gaul, 600 B.C.

Octavia —
Rome, 500 B.C.

Gertrude —
Germany, 500 B.C.

Malina —
Greece, 451 B.C.

La Donna Catarina —
Venice, 959.

Angelique —
France, 1250.

Elise —
France, 1350.

Giovanna Cenami and
Giovanni Arnolfini —
Flanders, 1434.

Mary of Burgundy
and Maximilian —
Burgundy and Austria, 1477.

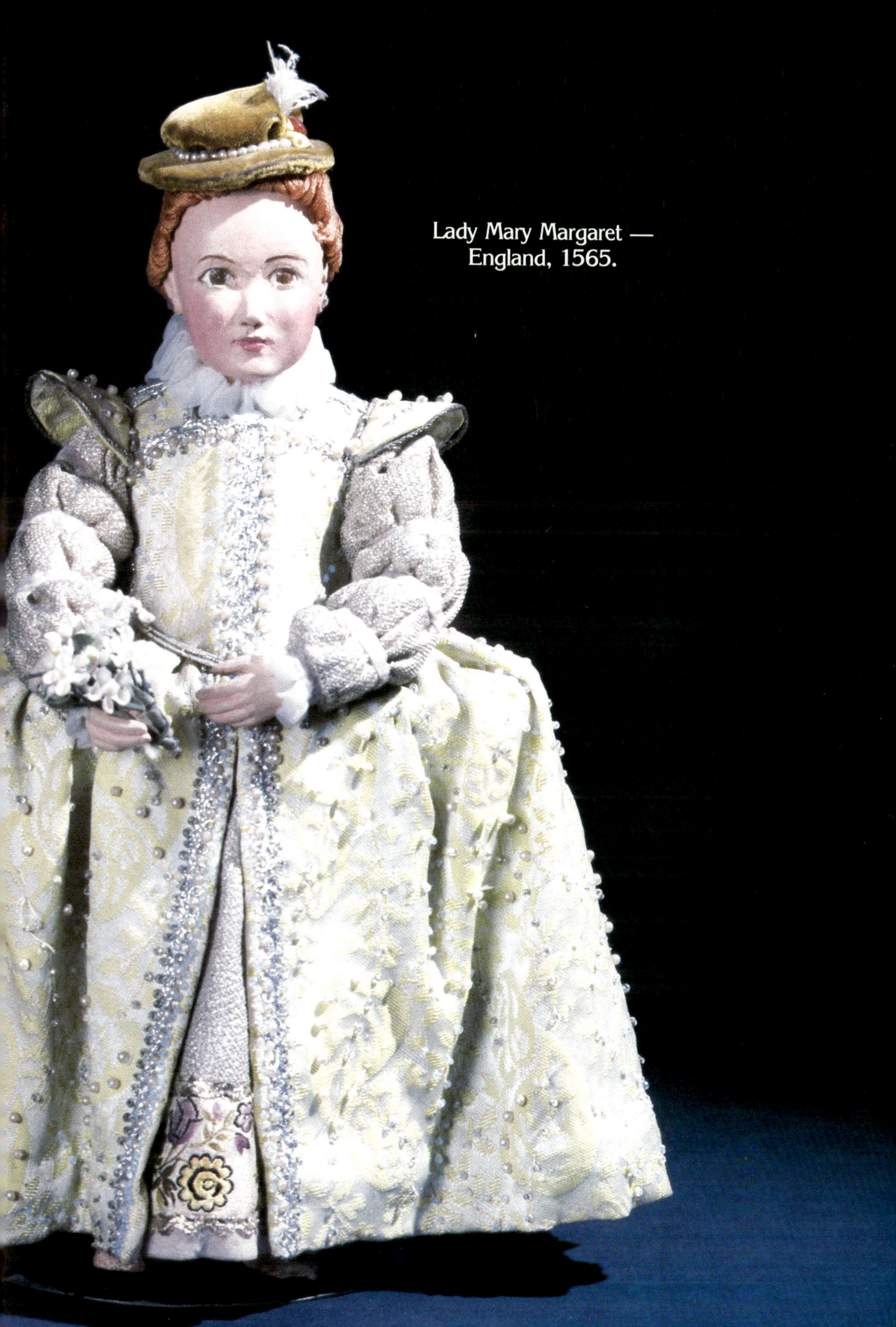

Lady Mary Margaret —
England, 1565.

Marie Louise —
France, 1720.

cummin, bay leaves, two pounds of lard, one pound of soft cheese; knead well. Bake on bay leaves."

Early Roman jewelry was simple and useful. Gold, silver and bronze pins, somewhat like big safety pins, were used to fasten their flowing robes — either plain or decorated with beads, polished pebbles or gold wire scroll. They were important accessories. Men and women wore gold, silver or bronze wire bracelets and iron, copper, brass or bronze rings.

In public, her matron's dress was greeted with profound respect. Men gave way to her in the street and in public places, the origin of our "ladies first."

Her own birthday was sacredly observed as a joyous occasion and the Matronalia, the Roman Mother's Day, was a national holiday, celebrated March 1st with a public festival.

With marriage, the Roman woman achieved a position superior to any others in the ancient world. She was absolute mistress in her home and a devoted wife and mother.

Although most Romans had slaves, she supervised her children and began training her daughters in the domestic arts from the time they were nine. It was a point of honor to have them well prepared for marriage and she would have considered it a great disgrace if a son-in-law complained that her daughter had been badly trained.

The women of the early Roman republic exerted a strong, beneficent influence on the family and nation, providing an inspiring example to women of all times. It is unfortunate that they fell from grace with the loose morality and luxuries of the Empire.

GERTRUDE

Germany, 500 B.C.

Gertrude means Spear Maiden and she illustrates marriage by purchase, but women were held in highest regard and respect as mothers of the race.

In the land between the Danube and the North Sea, there were the Germans, Jutes, Saxons, Franks, Goths, Lombards and Angles, all competing for space to live.

The Germans were a migratory people with vast herds, rapidly exhausting the land. When they moved to a new area, it had to be conquered by the sword. It was their way of life. "Degen," an old word for sword also meant warrior; it was a symbol of male virility. Boys were "degen kind," that is the children of the swords. They were fed their first solid food from its point.

They cherished freedom and believed that a glorious death in battle was preferable to captivity, for such a death insured a perpetual happy future life. They also believed that all husbands and wives leading virtuous lives on earth would never part again in Valhalla's heavenly halls.

As a result of all of this moving about, the women had great physical strength and beauty; they would fight beside their husbands in battle. It was sometimes said that a spinster must kill at least one enemy before she could marry. The women would fight to the death before being taken alive and they would kill each other, or if deprived of their swords, would strangle themselves with their long hair. (Later some would surrender with their children and them-

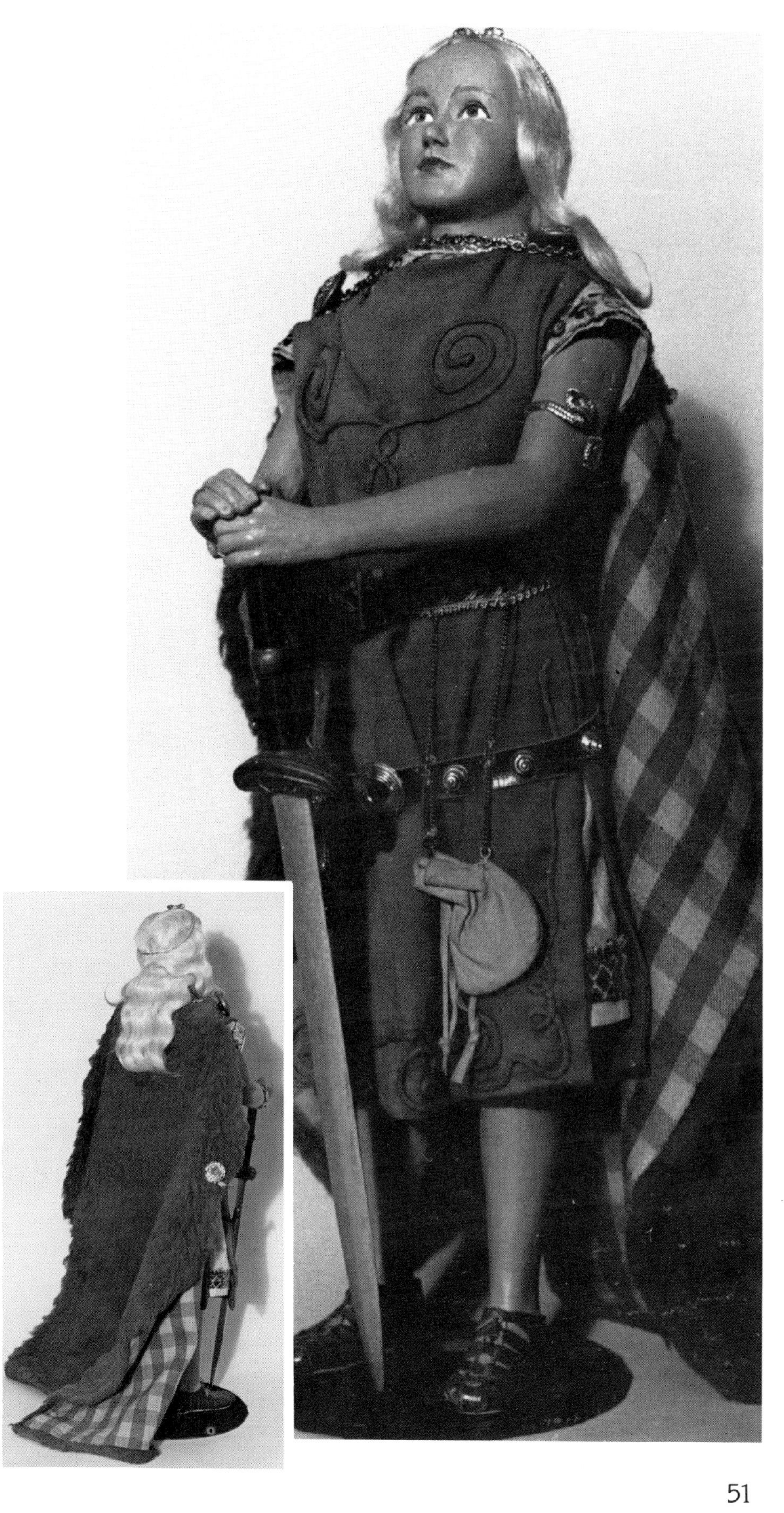

selves if they were promised to be made slaves of the Vestal Virgins.)

Their ideal of feminine virtue was the Goddess Frigga, patroness of the home and marriage. She, too, was equipped with a spear, shield and sword "to protect the home and carry the warriors to heaven." She was supposed to be blonde-haired and have blue eyes, the Teutonic ideal of beauty.

The Germans held that according to their ancient laws, only virgins could marry. From this arose the custom of the "morning gift," still extant among many European nations, to the bride from her husband as a reward for her chastity.

A bride was purchased from her father by a gift of cattle, horses and weapons. A man must consult his parents, her family, the tribal council and chiefs regarding marriage. Sometimes the bride-price was distributed amongst them.

Costume

Maidens wore tunics of green linen embroidered with red wool and under them a woolen tabard, open at the sides. The cape was secured on the shoulders by large gold brooches.

Long flowing hair indicates Gertrude was born free as well as a virgin. The circlet on her head symbolizes her rank, the daughter of a chieftain. There are embroidered red and green decorations in circles on the tabard. The woven belt illustrates her ability at embroidery. Her bearskin robe is lined with brilliant woolen plaid. She may even have killed and skinned the bear herself.

Her handsome leather girdle with the gold bosses is as was worn by Frigga. She wears a gold bracelet set with unfaceted gems. Her cloak clasp with circlet design represents Odin's snakes, a protective symbol.

Chains attached to the belt support the weight of the pouch which contains uncut jewels, her sewing instruments and a key. Her hunting knife fits neatly into its scabbard. Her handsome jewelry was massive and her gold collar, called a "torque," was another mark of rank. All of these motives show a fine sense of design for a comparatively primitive people.

Her wedding ring, copied from an ancient Saxon one, was received at the betrothal and worn on the right hand; no ring was used at the marriage ceremony.

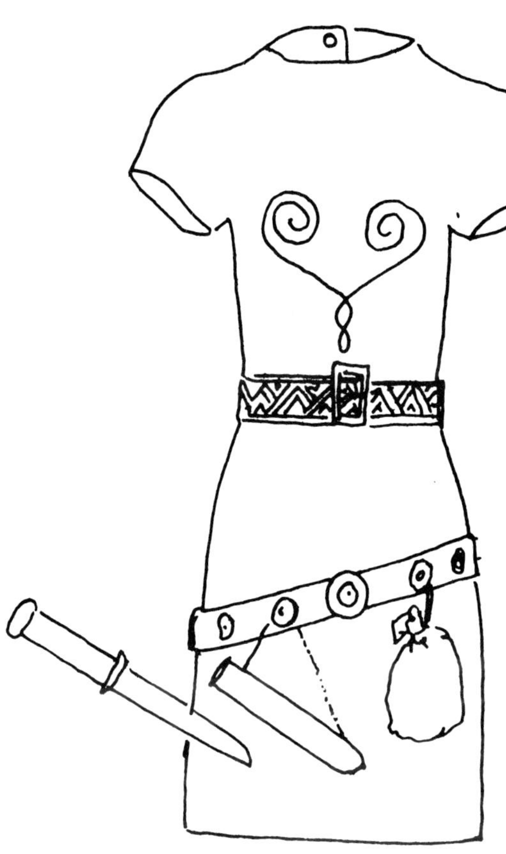

Knife and leather bag held
by loose leather belt.

Green linen tunic with red belt
embroidered red over white.

Small crown for chieftain's daughter.

Stout leather shoes.
No stockings.

Pair of gold brooches to hold cape.

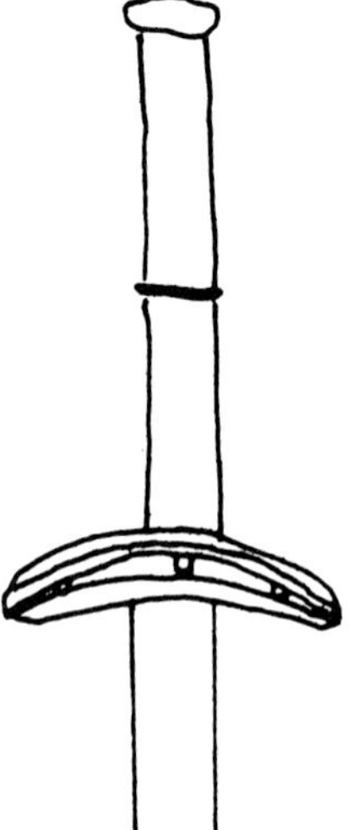

Two-handed broadsword.

Red and green embroidered
woolen tabard.

Customs

The wedding was in the tribal council and had some religious significance, for among the deities always invoked were Frigga, goddess of marriage and childbirth, and Thor, god of fire and life. His hammer was a sacred symbol and the marriage vows were sworn on it.

It was a family institution to have the father as a small priest.

The groom's gift to the bride was a two-handed, two-edged broadsword, shield and spear. In turn, she presented him with a gift of arms. Together they received a yoke of oxen and horses.

These Teutonic tribes showed a greater readiness to accept the Christian view of mankind, with the exaltation of the Blessed Virgin and the many women saints and martyrs than did the pagan communities of southern Europe because the northern countries had already paid such high honor to women.

They also worshipped in sacred groves, with ceremonies conducted by priests and priestesses.

They were a hearty people and their wedding feasts consisted of roast oxen and whole broiled salmon, cakes and sweets for the women and mead, fermented honey wine, for all.

Their custom of drinking mead for a moon after the wedding gave us our "honny moon," a pleasant term for a happy occasion, from the so-called barbarians!

MALINA

Greece, 451 B.C.

Malina represents the restricted marriage of the Greeks during the Golden Age of Pericles when each city and city-state had its own government and laws. Each was jealous of the other and worked constantly to remain strong and free. In 451 B.C. in an effort to stabilize and strengthen the state, curb the weakening influence of too many marriages and foreigners and reserve for Athens the material rewards of citizenship, the city permitted legal marriages only between its citizens.

Most Greek girls married at 14, 15 or 16 and it was customary for them to dedicate their dolls, toys and a lock of their hair to Artemis on the eve of their wedding. Here is a charming dedication of a young girl of the period: "Timarete, before her marriage, has offered up to Artemis her tambourine, and her valued ball, and her cap, defender of her locks, and her dolls, as is fitting for a virgin to a virgin, and her dolls' dresses. And do thou, oh Artemis, place thy hand over the girl Timarete and preserve holily her who is holy."

Costume

Greek brides of this period wore pink and this is the classic Doric chiton, trimmed with woven bands of the Greek key motif. It is held at the shoulders and sides with beautiful gold brooches or ivory pins and falls in elegant folds from the shoulders. Gold weights hang from the four corners of the overlap. Working to this scale, the folds had to be wired so that they would hang properly. This was the chiton supposedly worn by Artemis, the virgin goddess of the moon, so all Greek brides wore the virgin's chiton.

Sometimes they wore it alone or over the more complicated pleated Ionic chiton whose sleeves were held together with rows of small gold pins. It was also trimmed with embroidered bands. As we wanted to show both styles, we had her wear both. Both are of silk chiffon, duplicating the type fabric used by the Greeks. The silver trim at the bottom would have been done by a goldsmith who worked thin threads of gold and silver into the fabric, giving it weight and helping the drapery to hang properly.

Greek brides wove their fine white wedding veils and they wore handsome tiaras called "stephanes," also necklaces, bracelets and earrings. Malina's wedding ring was worn on the third finger of the left hand, following a superstition brought from the East that a vein ran directly from that finger to the heart. Many wedding rings had inscriptions on the inside. We like the one that says simply, Honey." Good taste required restraint. The bride's gold leather sandals with beautiful designs were in fashion and comfortable.

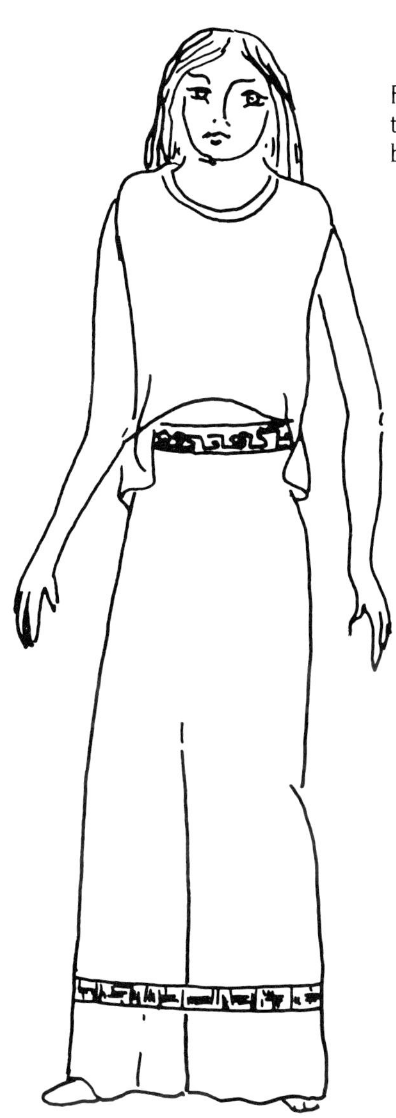

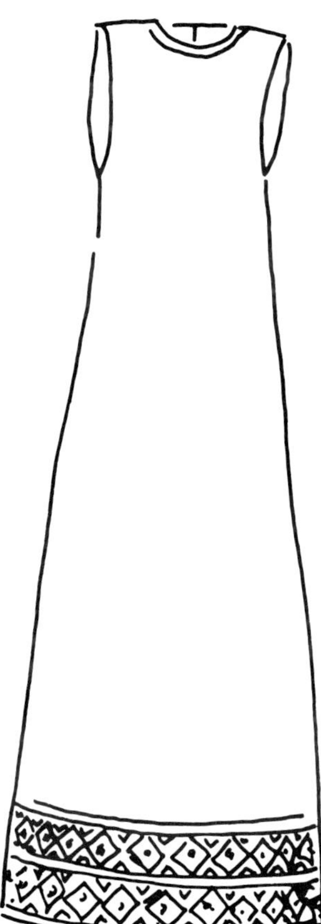

Doric
Fine chiffon garment with silver threads worked into the lower skirt by goldsmiths.

Linen undergarment with embroidery.

Typical early Greek earrings.

Ionic
Chiffon costume with gold pins
and design on the lower skirt.

Gold tiara.

Early bracelet.

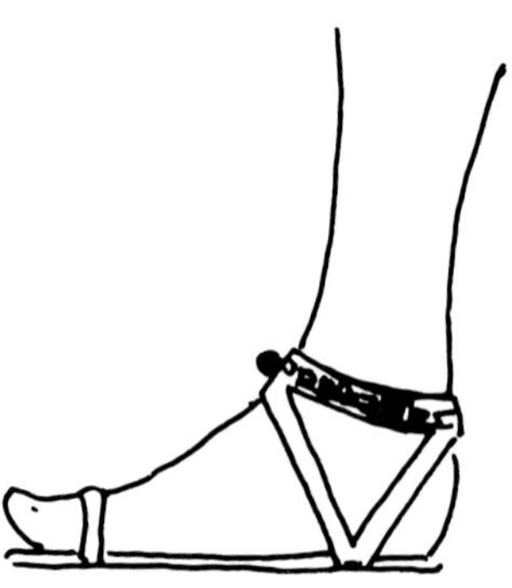

Golden leather sandals.

Customs

Girls were taught to read, write, play an instrument, weave and embroider; however, they were kept in almost Oriental seclusion and also to "see as little, hear as little and ask as few questions as possible, the most important lesson being MODESTY."

Demosthenes said, "We have courtesans for the sake of pleasure, concubines for the daily health of our bodies, and wives to bear us lawful offspring and to be the faithful guardians of our homes."

Most men did not marry for love (often waiting until they were 35), but to continue themselves and the State through a suitably dowered wife and to have children to ward off the evil fate of an untended soul in the hereafter. The young wife lived quietly in her new home, praying that her first child would be a boy, but feeling secure in the knowledge that as a legal wife, her children, her home and her husband's estates were to be in her hands when he died.

Some Greeks were blonde and blue-eyed, a coloring very much admired. Men and women who were not natural blondes sometimes dyed their hair or wore wigs made from the coveted golden tresses gotten from the captured barbarians.

Many men loved their wives and there are many fine examples of marital fidelity, as shown by this epitaph from the second century: "Under this stone Marathonis laid his Nicopolisi to rest and spilled tears upon the marble coffin. They were useless, for what remains for a man whose wife has departed, leaving him alone in the world?"

Themistocles, the famous Greek general and statesman said, "The Athenians govern the Greeks, I govern the Athenians, you wife, govern me, and our son governs you, let him then use with moderation that power, which, child as he is, sets him above all the Greeks."

Marriages were arranged by the parents and the girl had no say, docilely accepting the man who was selected for her.

All Greek weddings were preceded by a formal legal ceremony of betrothal and the bestowal of the dowry in the presence of witnesses. Athenian wedding rites included bathing in the sacred spring of Kallichoran to ensure children and offerings to the gods of marriage and Athens, patron goddess of the city. While not consid-

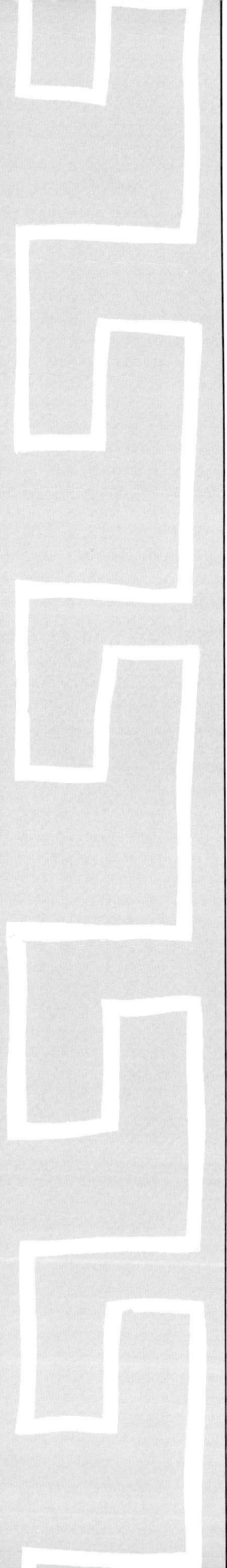

ered a sacrament, their wedding ceremony had deep religious significance.

At the wedding feast in the bride's home, the men sat on one side of the room and the women on the other, while wedding cake, sweetmeats and wine were served. Festivities concluded in the early evening when the groom escorted his veiled bride by carriage, accompanied with music and songs, to his parents' home, where they welcomed her.

The bridal couple stopped at the door to receive the new fire at an altar erected there, after which the carriage was burned, symbolizing the bride's severance of all ties with her family. The groom carried her over the threshold, commemorating marriage by capture. Both ate a piece of quince before entering the house, "so that all may be sweetness between them," and also to remind them to protect each other, as the quince was supposed to be an antidote for poisons.

The guests escorted the couple to the bridal bedroom and gathered outside the door to sing the epithalamion or marriage chamber song followed by boisterous talk and sometimes crude jokes until the groom announced that the marriage had been consummated.

The next day, known as "the unveiling," the bridal couple received their friends who brought gifts and were entertained with another wedding feast.

In earlier ages, Greek women were on a higher plane and had more education than at this time, when the family pattern had gradually changed from the maternal to the paternal order.

This led men to seek female companionship outside the home and to the rise of the hetarae, or mistresses, who were usually foreigners, chiefly Oriental. Witty, intelligent and stimulating intellectually and physically, they catered to the Athenian man's new-found interest in the pleasures of the intellect as well as those of the body. This was very similar to the Japanese geisha, except that the Greeks included the physical aspect of the relationship which the geisha do not. The sophisticated hetarae, in their transparent flowered robes, were an exotic contrast to the decorous naive young wives.

LA DONNA CATARINA

Venice, 959

La Donna Catarina, Venice, 959 A.D. will represent Christian group marriage. Historians believe that these marriage customs give credit to the Venetian's claim to descent from the Babylonians. It does seem logical.

Costume

Noble Venetian brides were richly dressed in handsome imported Eastern fabrics trimmed with sable, ermine, gold and jewels. The gold threads in their flowing hair were symbols of virginity.

Although Venetians followed the Byzantine fashion of wearing richly jeweled rings, brooches and cloak clasps, their engagement rings were plain gold bands.

Catarina wears a handsome mink-trimmed silk and wool white cape over her beautifully patterned gold colored Eastern silk tunic. Under it is the traditional white robe trimmed with heavy gold braid. Under her robe she has a lace-trimmed linen shift and soft cloth-of-gold slippers over white silk hose.

Her sheer veil indicates a wife's dependence on her husband and obedience to his will. Over the veil she wears the small gold bridal crown, symbolic of the Virgin Queen of Heaven.

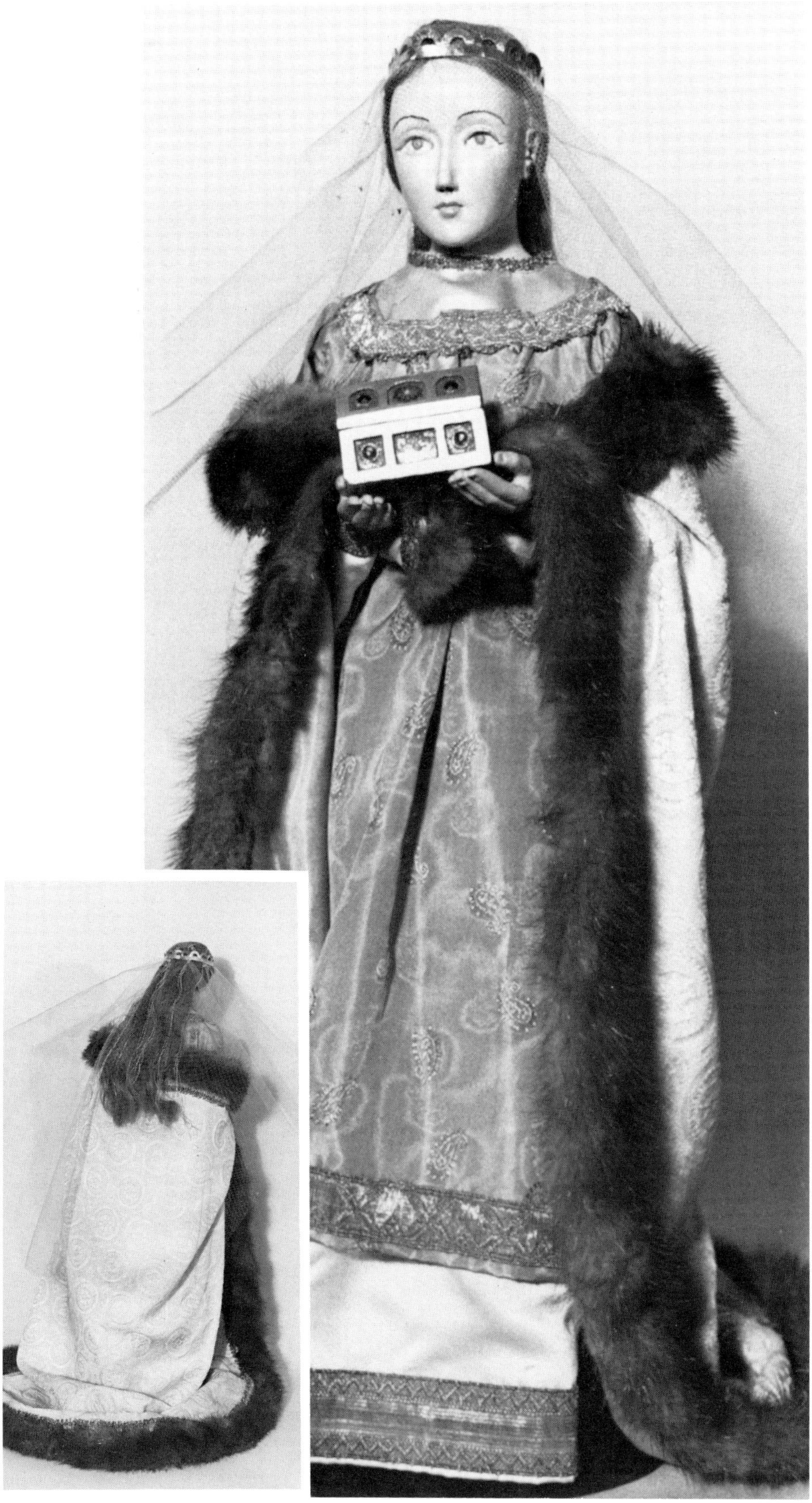

65

Customs

Catarina's marriage was arranged by her parents and the groom's but her courtship, betrothal and marriage customs were in the most romantic and elegant Venetian traditions.

One of the most charming was the customary "good luck" betrothal gift exchanged and worn by the happy couple — delicate little gold chains, made especially for the purpose by Venetian goldsmiths.

For centuries all Venetian weddings were held on January 31st — nobles one year, tradesmen and commoners the next.

At the noble wedding the brides stood in a circle around the High Altar, holding their arcella (little arcs) filled with gold and jewels. Their families waited at the rear of the cathedral for the arrival of the grooms accompanied by the "sponsors of the ring," their best men.

At the ceremony the Bishop blessed the young couples and each groom slipped the symbolic ring, the same style for all, on his bride's finger. After that, the brides left gifts of virgin wax for candles for the cathedral; each groom gave a sum of money "in proportion to his opinion of his wife's beauty." This money formed a fund from which poor brides of the people received dowries the following year. Their best men took gifts of rare liqueurs and rich wines, and the next morning, they gave the bridal couples symbolic gifts of fresh eggs for fertility and aromatic pastries for sweetness and harmony, a relic from the Greek's "eating of the quince."

We chose the date of 959 for this Venetian bride because that was the year of the great bridal kidnapping!

The Venetians had been feuding with a group of Istrian pirates from the north and the pirates, knowing the annual marriage custom, decided to carry off the brides and their dowries. The night before the ceremony the corsairs ran their light sailing vessels under the shelter of the island where the Venetian Arsenal now stands and secreted themselves near the cathedral.

The next morning, after the brides and their families were assembled, the pirates rushed into the cathedral, shouting and brandishing their swords. As most of the fathers were elderly and all were unarmed, this surprise attack enabled the pirates to carry off the brides to their waiting ships and quickly sail away.

Silk damask tunic with gold galloon edgings, silk lined.

Gold bridal crown.

Lace-trimmed natural linen chemise lined with silk.

Small gold casket for DOT.

When the bridegrooms arrived, they found such weapons as they could and led by the Doge in his state robes, they all rushed to the nearest boats and rowed furiously after the pirates who were still in sight.

The morning breeze failed and although the pirates took to their oars, they were no match for the enraged bridegrooms. A sea battle followed, all of the pirates were killed, all the brides and their dower chests rescued and all returned safely to the cathedral and were married "before the sun marked noon."

The immediate result of this attack was a series of successful expeditions against the pirates, laying the foundation for Venetian power on the mainland — an important turning point in the history of Venice, all because of the kidnapped brides.

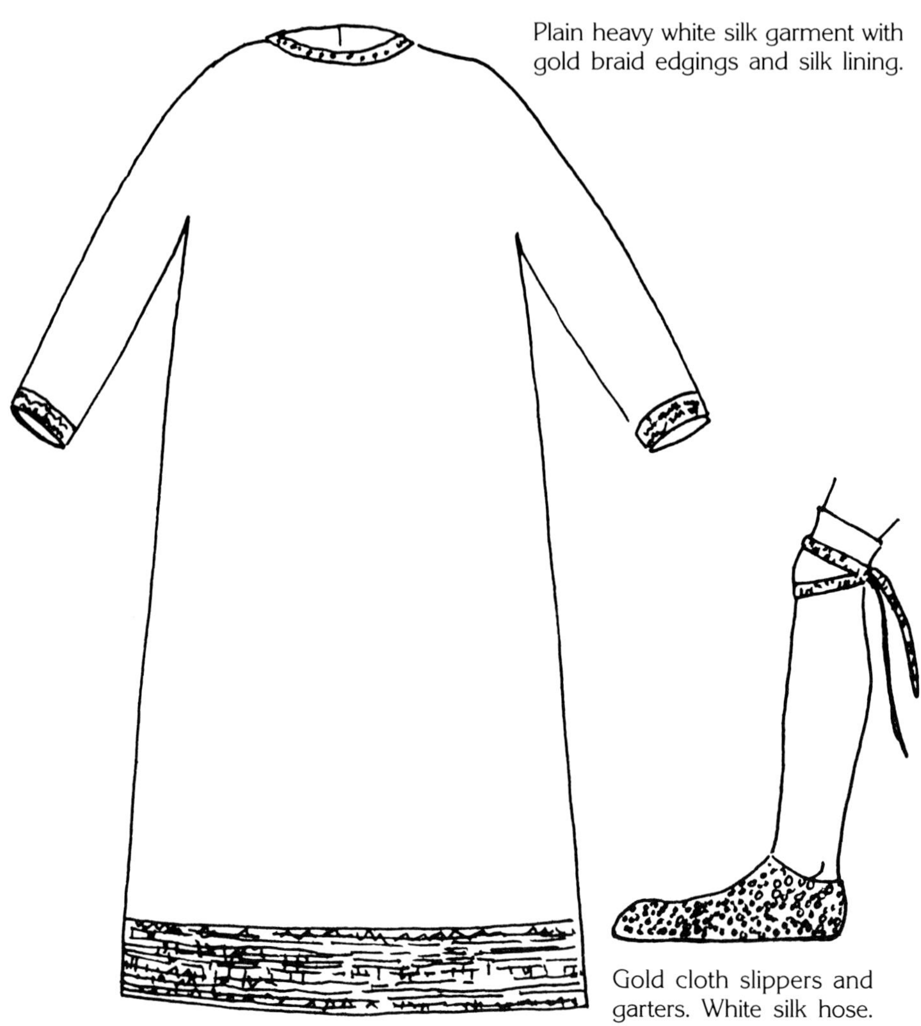

Plain heavy white silk garment with gold braid edgings and silk lining.

Gold cloth slippers and garters. White silk hose.

ANGELIQUE

France, 1250

Angelique represents marriage at the church door. Her date is approximately 1250 A.D.

Costume

The beautiful simple lines of her costume lasted undated for more than 100 years. The magnificent Eastern fabrics introduced into Europe by the crusaders combined to make these garments worthy of being handed down from generation to generation, as they were.

Angelique models the three main parts of the 13th century dress: mantle, robe and under robe. The mantle's deep, rich sapphire blue is a color as characteristic of the French at that time as purple was of the Imperial Romans. It was also the color of the Virgin's robe, the Bride of Heaven, and this time it became a favorite color for brides. (We were told by a gentleman who recently attended a wedding in Paris that the bride wore a cape, identical so far as he could see, to this, and that it had been in her family for more than 600 years!) The changeable taffeta lining was another feature and was originally called "shot silk."

Her robe is beautifully cut and the real gold thread, natural dyes and pure silk made it very costly. It would be not only her bridal gown, but also worn on state occasions. It has a train, the fashion of the Middle Ages that almost drove the clergy wild. The Church preached violently against any fashion change and one irate monk thundered, "Even the Devil is content with only one tail," for women wore trains on their mantles and under robes as well as on their gowns.

Her soft blue silk under robe repeats a bride's favorite color which was also symbolic of the sky and God's protection. Under it she wears a fine white linen chemise.

The heavily jeweled (with large stones) girdle was an accessory. It was believed that jewels had magic powers to protect health, preserve love and ease childbirth, so girdles became a preferred place to display handsome jewels, remaining in fashion for many years.

Angelique also wears the three main adornments of a medieval bride: the ring for eternal vows and true love; the brooch for modesty and a clean heart; the garland, crown of virtue, for "successfully resisting temptation." The Church encouraged girls to cherish the privilege of wearing the bridal garland as one of their

highest honors. Sometimes a girl would be given the garlands of maiden friends. On remarriage, no woman was permitted to wear the garland or the brooch.

Her veil symbolizes woman's dependence on her husband and her submission to his will. Her flowing hair indicates free birth and virginity. Sheer veils and visible hair are innovations of this period, when hair and attractive head coverings were accented. Matilda, a freeborn Saxon princess who had beautiful hair which she refused to hide, helped to make it appreciated.

Previously, the Church required that a woman's hair be hidden under heavy, opaque coverings because it was considered too seductive. These changes in hairdressing and head covering were medieval woman's signs of her new freedom.

Angelique has interesting footwear; her red velvet shoes covered with gold mesh embroidered with pearls indicate her rank. Her hose were smartly tailored and well fitting. Sometimes they had front and back seams. Her garters were sometimes aided by another at mid thigh, attached by ribbons to a belt around the waist, so you see ours are not new.

She carries sprays of gilded wheat, a symbol of fertility. After the ceremony, she shook the grains from the stalks and young girls scrambled for them and tossed them at her for good luck, as we do rice, confetti, rose petals or bird seed. Sometimes the grains were saved, ground and baked into small thin biscuits which were broken over the bride's head at the wedding feast as a good luck token. In some parts of Scotland this is still done.

At court, charming marzipan figures were used for decorating wedding cakes. They were also sold in the streets of Paris.

Oriental silk brocade gown with soft blue silk under robe.
Jeweled cuffs and girdle. Crown of flowers. Heavy veil
edged with gold embroidery.

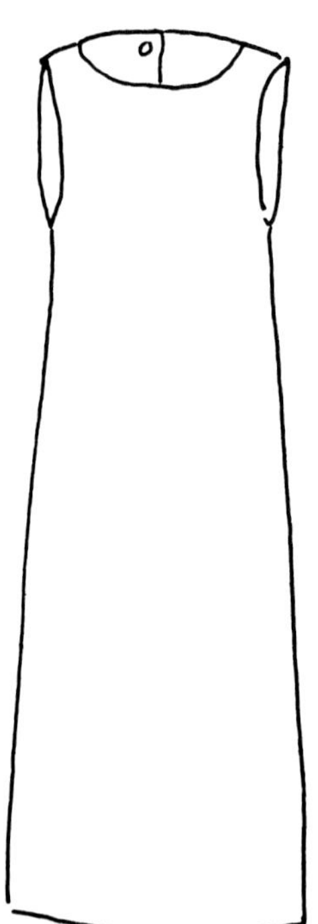

White linen chemise.

Soft blue silk under robe with train.

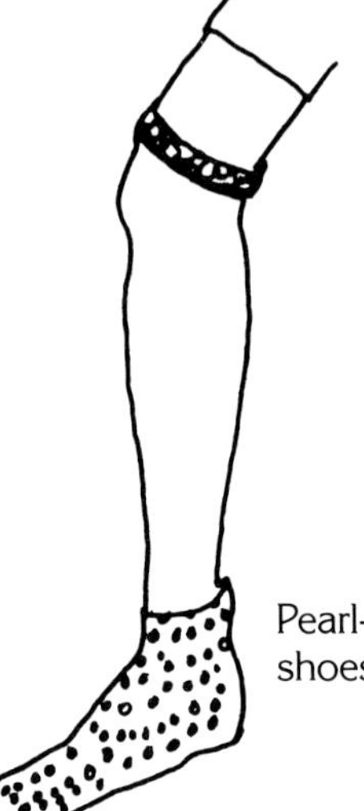

Pearl-trimmed red velvet
shoes. White stockings.

Customs

Angelique represents marriage at the church porch or doorway, a custom which prevailed until 1560, for religious and legal reasons. Due to the physical aspects of marriage, the Church felt it unsuitable to exchange the wedding vows inside the sacred building.

Legally, the terms of the dower were declared publicly prior to the ceremony so that all guests witnessing this important agreement could attest to it later if necessary.

After the ceremony, the wedding party went inside for the wedding mass and sermon; however, the actual marriage was not performed in the Church until after the reformation.

As a compensation for this restriction, one very charming part of the ceremony was when the groom blessed the ring. After receiving it from the priest, carefully holding it between the thumb and forefinger, he held it over the thumb, saying, "In the name of the Father," then over the index fingers, "and of the Son," then over the middle finger, "and of the Holy Spirit," then over the fourth finger, "Amen."

The groom also observed the traditional custom of presenting the bride with a sou and a dernier, representing the ancient bride-price. If a girl was married with the ring and the money, it was much more difficult to dissolve the union.

While the Church encouraged marriage for the sake of the family, it clung to the early Christian belief that women were unclean and inferior and should be continually punished for Eve's fall.

During the 13th century, Louis IX, who was a prestigious dresser, helped France soften the severity to women in two ways — first, by fostering the growing worship of the Virgin Mary and second, by encouraging the institution of chivalry. He helped to make France the leader of the fashion world. Socially, women were now on a pedestal, a gradual change from the sinful Eve to pure Madonna was effected. Woman now symbolized man's consecration to his knightly vows to protect the weak, encourage virtue and live his religion. Each knight's lady became his personal Madonna.

Socially, things were vastly improved. Legally, women's lives were completely controlled by men. A girl could not yet choose her

own husband; this remained the right of her nearest male guardian. Romantic love seldom entered into the marriage arrangements; if the couple was in love, they were just very lucky.

The marriage of a wealthy heiress was usually controlled by the reigning prince, who rewarded this rich prize to a faithful follower.

There were many marriages due to the crusades and frequent wars, large and small. Many attacks on castles resulted in the victor marrying the defeated noble's widow, sister, ward or daughter. There was no scarcity of husbands. Our word "husband" comes from this time. Originally, it was "hus" (house) "bunda" (owner). Under feudal law, most men, particularly serfs, could not own homes. However, free-holders of the yeoman class were permitted to own a house and a few acres of land as a reward for military service. Ambitious mothers were anxious for their daughters to win "house owners" and by the 13th century, the word came to mean any man joined in marriage, whether he owned a home or not. So the 13th century can be credited for the better attitude toward women.

LE DEMOISELLE ELISE

France, 1350

La Demoiselle Elise, France, circa 1350 A.D. represents a bride in wardship, a feudal law which gave their overlord the power to arrange the marriage of heiresses upon the death of their male relatives.

# Costume

The cote-hardie was the traditional wedding gown of the Middle Ages. Many were of handsome, costly fabrics, handed down by will from mother to daughter. Girls who did not inherit one would rent one for the important occasion. Close-fitting through the body, long sleeved, with a graceful voluminous skirt, it was a very flattering fashion.

Elise has a richly patterned floral brocade gown whose long sleeves are trimmed with gold buttons. The girdle was an important and costly accessory and this one with gold links alternating with enameled and jeweled flowers is worn low on the hips in the latest fashion. Under it she wears a full length, finely pleated chemise trimmed with embroidery and under that a heavier linen short smock. She would also wear a form of closely fitting corset, usually of soft suede, laced up the back.

Her cloth hose are carefully fitted, gartered with ribbons and the velvet shoes are sewed with jewels.

Noble brides of this period wore lovely little jeweled caps instead of veils and always had flowing hair, indicating virginity.

Her wedding ring is a handsome ruby set in gold. She carries white flowers in her skirt with which she will decorate the altar of the family chapel.

Brides were permitted only three dresses in their trousseau — the wedding gown, which would also be worn for state occasions and great feasts, one dress for Sundays and holidays, and one for every day.

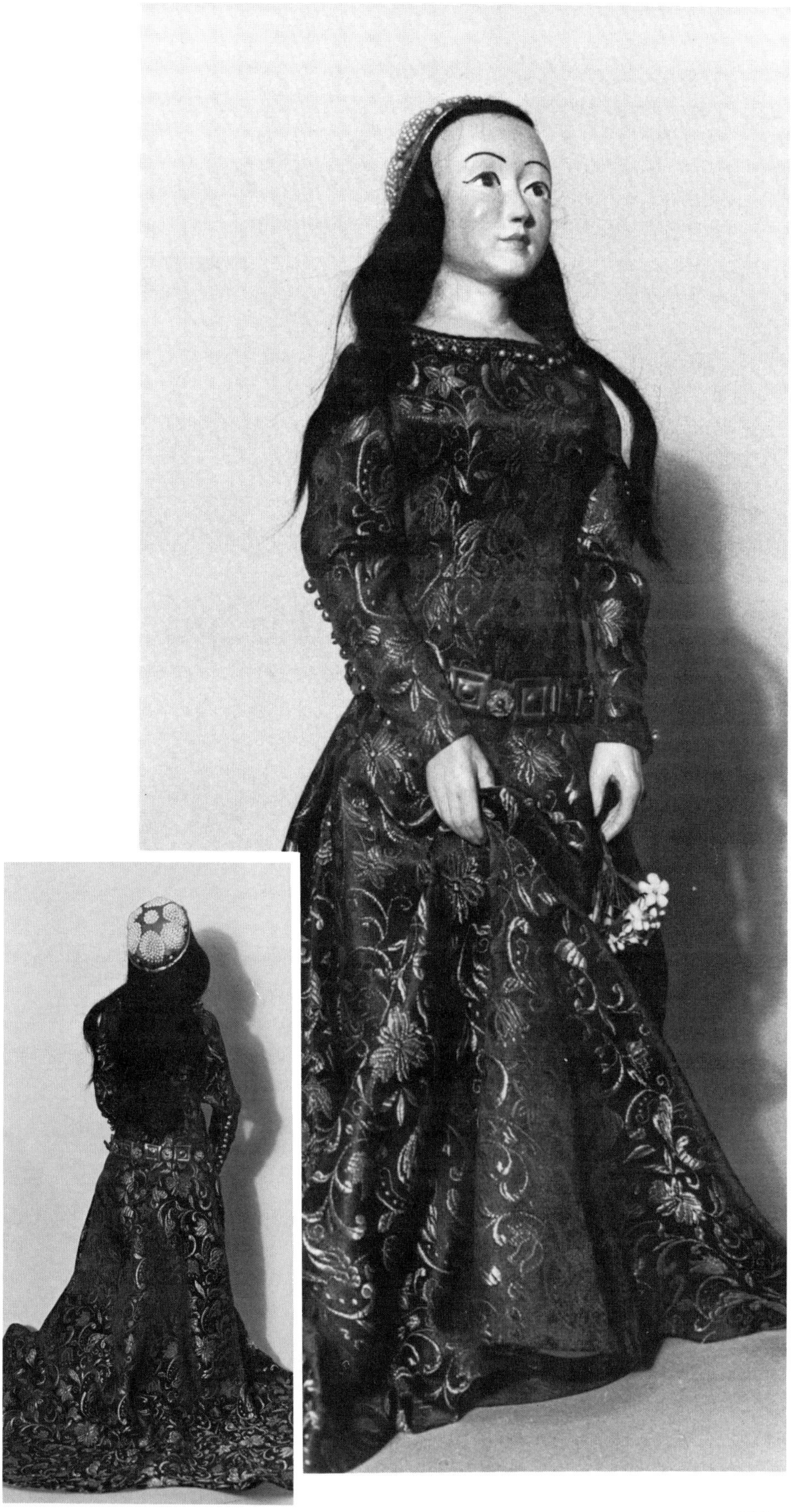

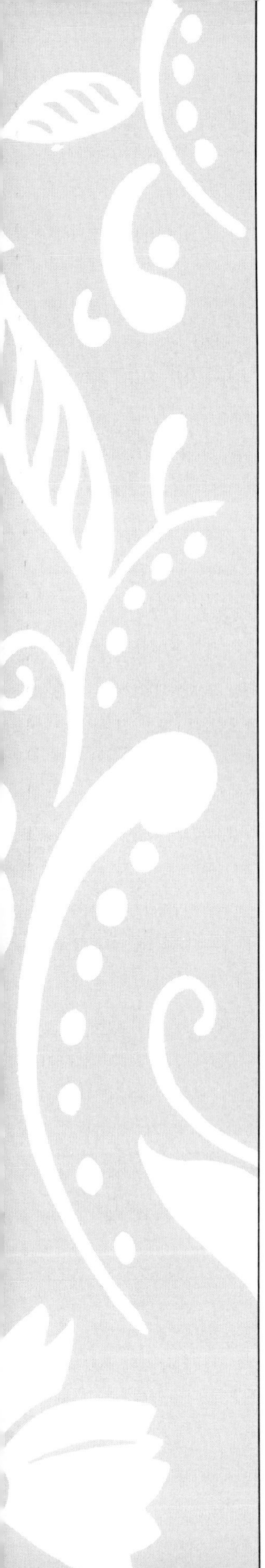

Customs

Under the laws of wardship, a woman and all of her property could be handed over to any man her sovereign wanted to reward or to win to his service. The only restraining factor was the "law of disparagement" which provided that women of noble families could not be given in marriage to men of lesser rank.

All heiresses, widows and maids, without male relatives, were recognized as vassals of the Crown. None of them could marry without the consent of the overlord who held wardship of their person and domains. If a woman did marry without the overlord's consent, she was liable to heavy fines and the forfeiture of her land and holdings, while her husband could be hung or beheaded for "disloyalty to the Crown."

Overlords could compel a woman in wardship to marry so that the military duties of her lands might be performed by a man. For example, a baron could say to such a ward, "Dame, you owe service of marriage," and then designate three suitable candidates among whom she must choose a husband. Since she could not go to war, she had to provide a husband who could. This was frequently done during the crusades, when an overlord wanted many strong knights and their followers in his retinue. He often filled vacancies this way.

These powers of wardship, given formally by law, were upheld by custom. Like many other customs, the system gradually degenerated and led to many abuses, governed by the whim or avarice of the overlord who forced many an unwilling ward into marriage.

Such overlords frequently sold the wardship to the highest bidder or suggested a completely impossible candidate, forcing the heiress to buy her freedom. He would say, "You will either marry this decrepit (sometimes senile or diseased) old knight, to whose rank and wealth you cannot possibly object, or you will pay me so much." Although old romances are filled with stories of the heiress-ward who renounced all for love, actually most wards had little choice but to submit to such blackmail.

Even in Elizabethan times the abuses of wardship were flagrant. An entire book has been written about Queen Elizabeth I's restrictions upon the ladies of her court who were in wardship to her.

Full-length embroidered linen chemise.

Girdle of gold and enameled links.

Jeweled cap.

Gold ring set with a ruby.

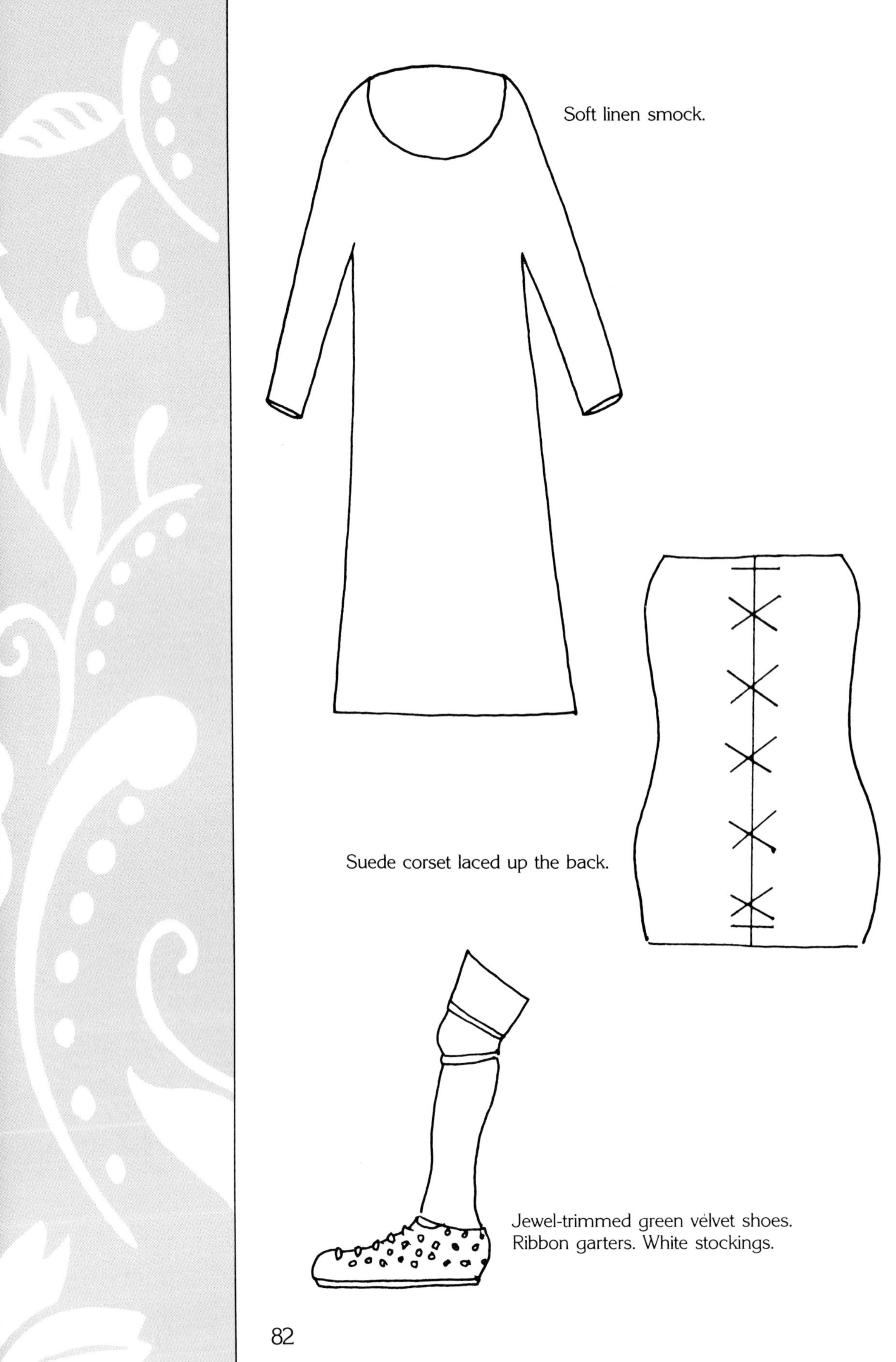

Soft linen smock.

Suede corset laced up the back.

Jewel-trimmed green velvet shoes.
Ribbon garters. White stockings.

GIOVANNA CENAMI

Flanders, 1434

Giovanna Cenami represents self-marriage with her husband, Giovanni Arnolfini, an Italian merchant, who lived in Bruges, Flanders, from 1420 to 1472. Their famous double portrait, painted in 1434 by Jan van Eyck, is probably a wedding certificate. The original is in the National Gallery in London. It is only 33in (84cm) tall, oil on wood, and is the largest picture he ever painted.

Ever since 700, the Christian Church has tried to uphold the sanctity of marriage, first, by providing a religious ceremony with a certain form — then in the 10th and 11th centuries, issuing edicts against civil marriage. Finally, in the 12th century, they made marriage the seventh sacrament and an indissoluble union.

Despite this, people continued to marry themselves under canon law, until 1563, when the Council of Trent ruled that a priest and two witnesses must be present, in an attempt to combat the abuses of self-marriage.

Up until this time, people could marry themselves privately if they wished, by observing the proper ceremony, which the couple in the painting are doing. Nearly everything about this picture pertains to marriage, law and religion.

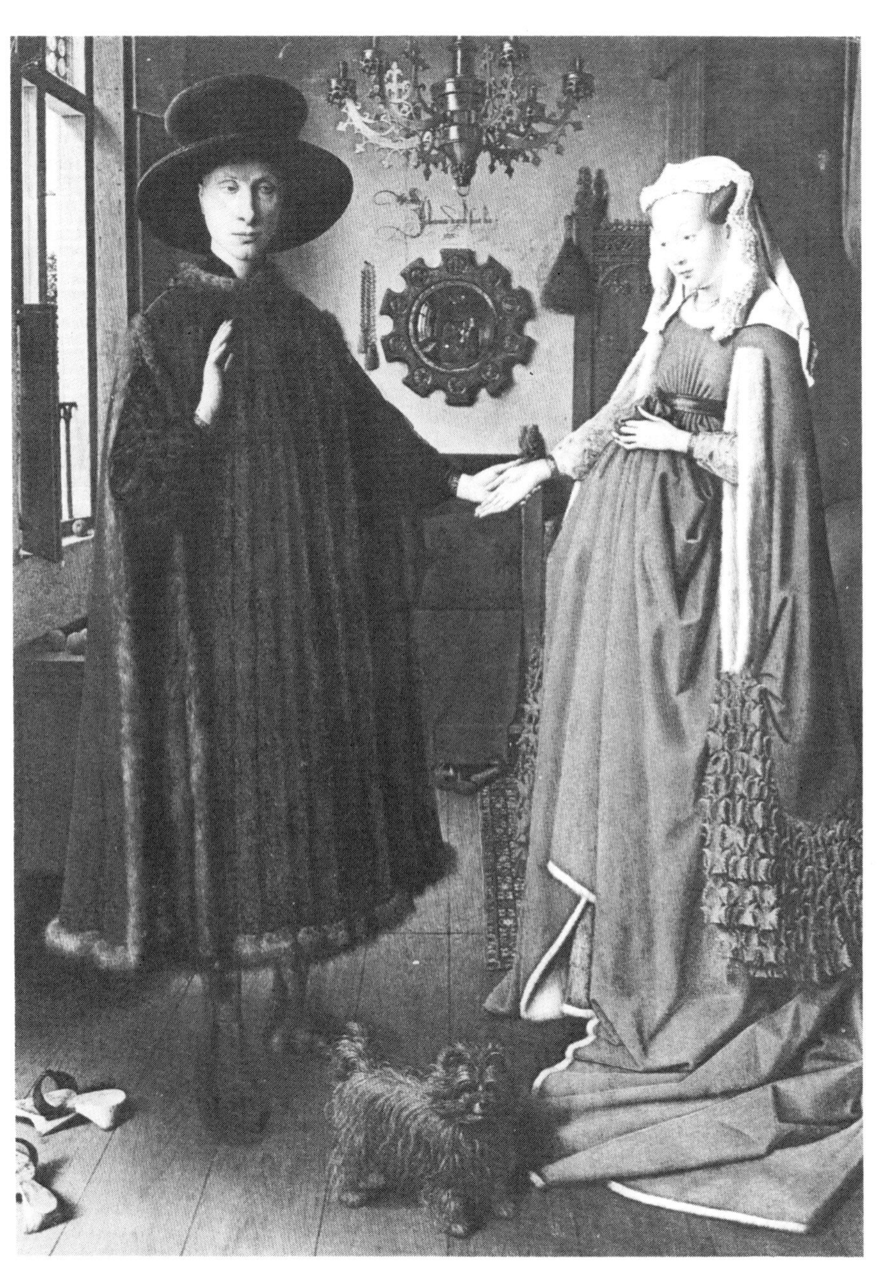

Betrothal of the Arnolfini painted in 1434 by Jan van Eyck. *National Gallery*, London.

Costume

Giovanna's green wool gown, lined with fur and silk, has long, full "bag" sleeves trimmed with rows of petals. (There are 221 on each sleeve. They must be sewed together in sets of ten; there is no other way to do it and have them look correct.)

Her blue silk under robe is also deeply lined with fur, under which she wears an embroidered fine linen chemise.

This bride's red and gold girdle is worn high under the bosom. Her long yellow hose are gartered by blue ribbons.

High foreheads were considered a mark of beauty. Women plucked out their front hair to achieve the desired effect. For her

unusual coiffure, the hair was parted in the middle and at the sides, over the ears. Then each front part was wrapped neatly around wire cones at the sides of the head, covered with fine gold mesh and held in place with a narrow plait around the base of the cone. The rest of the hair was gathered into a plaited bun at the back and helped anchor the intricately folded white linen coif with finely pleated frill.

The wedding ring was worn on the second joint of the third finger. It was probably engraved as mottos were now placed on wedding rings instead of on girdles. A favorite inscription for a bride was the likeness of St. Margaret, patron saint of women in childbirth, with the motto, "Be of good heart."

The groom's right hand is raised in solemn oath and he joins hands with his bride in the traditional wedding handclasp. A lighted candle, symbolic of the all-seeing eye of God, was required at all oaths, so one burns in the chandelier.

Above the mirror, in legal Latin script, the artist lettered, "Jan van Eyck was present" to attest he witnessed the ceremony. In the mirror he painted himself with another witness. Around the mirror, in its frame, are ten beautiful miniatures of Christ's passion. At the right of the mirror, the string of crystal beads, probably a rosary, symbolizes Marian purity.

The fruit on the windowsill represents man's innocence before "the Fall," and the finial on the chair, above the whisk, is a tiny statue of St. Margaret.

Note the bride's red wooden shoes. You will see in the picture that her husband has also removed his, following the Biblical injunction to "put off thy shoes for thou standest on holy ground," which was customary in this type of marriage. Here, also, is the little dog, symbol of marital fidelity.

Now to answer the question so often raised by this painting — no the bride is NOT pregnant. The illusion of pregnancy is due to the posture of the times, similar to the "debutante slouch" of the 1920s, and the fashionable bunching-up of the heavy trailing gowns over the abdomen. The fashion was exaggerated by some young married women, indicating a desired pregnancy. Due to wars and epidemics, 15th century Europe had a high death rate and a population explosion was encouraged.

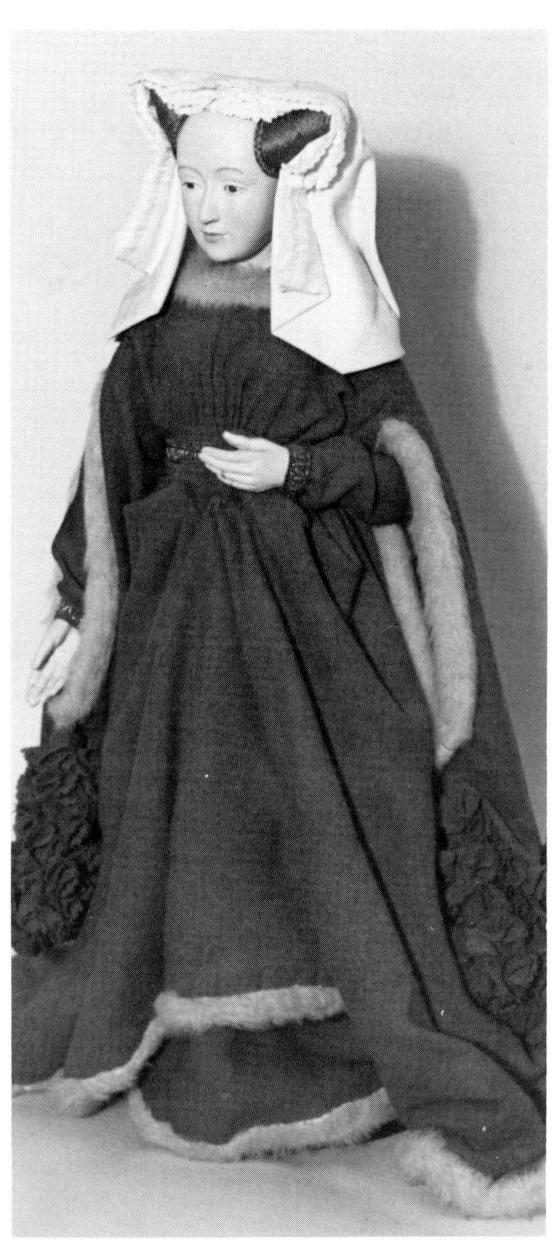

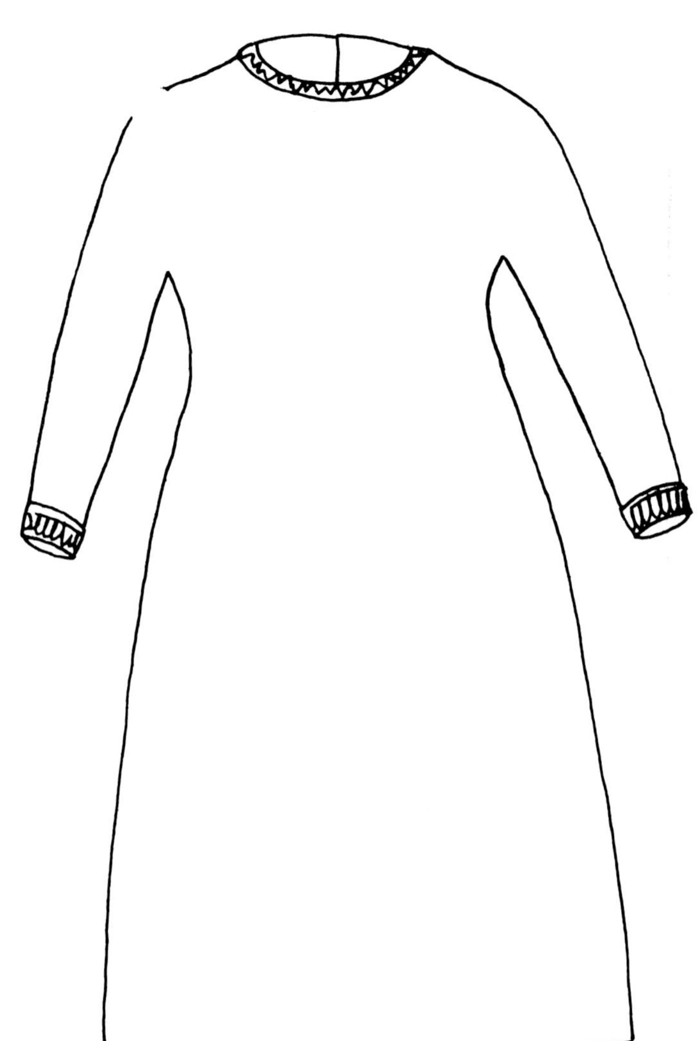

Blue silk under robe with red cuffs, deeply lined with fur.

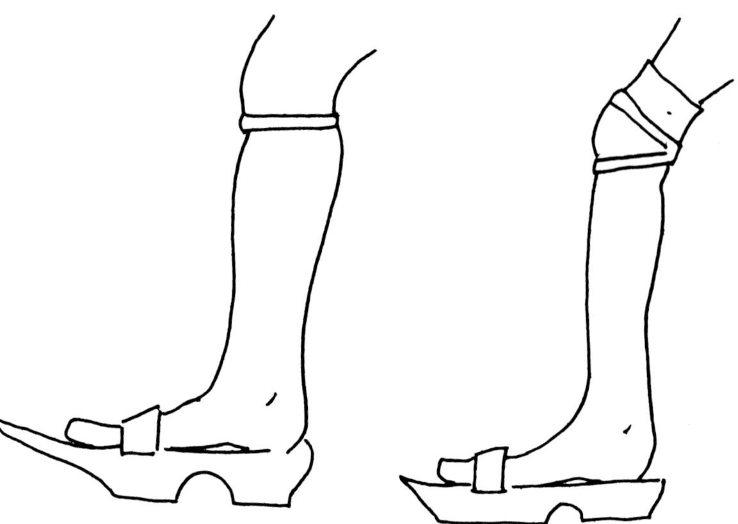

Black sandals and hose (his).

Red sandals and yellow hose gartered with blue ribbons (hers).

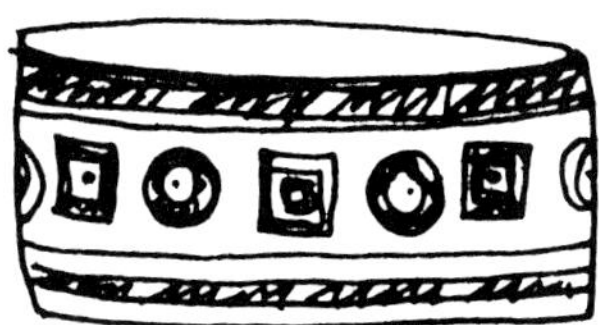

Red and gold girdle worn high under bosom.

Lace-trimmed linen chemise.

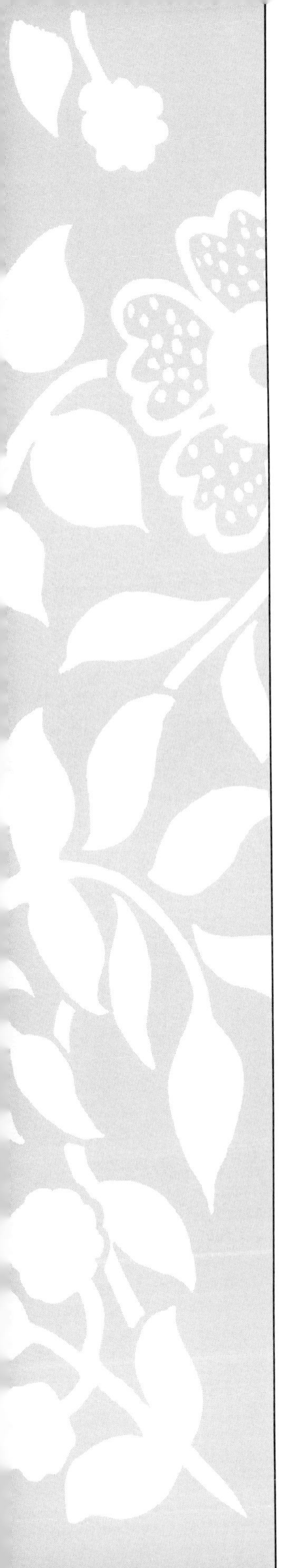

MARY OF BURGUNDY

Burgundy and Austria, 1477

Mary of Burgundy represents a royal marriage between two countries, Burgundy and Austria, August 18, 1477.

She was descended from a romantic ancestor, Philip the Good, who had founded the Order of the Golden Fleece in 1429. Mary, however, was very practical and finally, to foil the scheme of Louis XI who tried to obtain possession of her inheritance by becoming her guardian, she acceded to her father's wishes that she marry Maximilian of Austria.

Dr. William Moroltinger wrote to the Archduke Maximilian just before the engagement, "At the betrothal, your Grace must have a ring set with a diamond, and also a gold ring." This famous passage from the Vienna court records was one of the first instances specifying a diamond as an engagement ring.

We believe it was a happy marriage but Mary of Burgundy died as a result of a fall from her horse in March of 1482.

Costume

Mary of Burgundy is wearing a floral crown on a black cap and a somewhat similar necklace of carved gold flowers.

The brocade cloak is trimmed at the edges with white velvet and an embroidered band trimmed with gold bosses holds the cloak far enough apart to display the gown beneath, which is specially shaped with openings to let the arms of the blue gown beneath show through. The blue gown has white satin cuffs and wide embroidery at the bottom. Both are lined with white satin. White linen is worn next to the skin.

She wears red slippers, white stockings and gold ribbon garters.

Maximilian of Austria wears a dark Venetian velvet cloak with wide white velvet trimming at the edges. It is held together with a double gold chain.

His coat is of gold damask with a little bit of fur around the very casual-fitting neck. He wears a red belt with round gold bosses. His hat has a black velvet center surrounded by red and gold and decorated with a feather.

His hose are of dark red and black Venetian velvet, reaching down from the waist and trimmed with gold braid. Slippers are black with a swirling gold design.

Gold damask coat trimmed with fur around the neck. Red velvet belt with round gold bosses.

Black velvet hat with red and gold trimming and a feather.

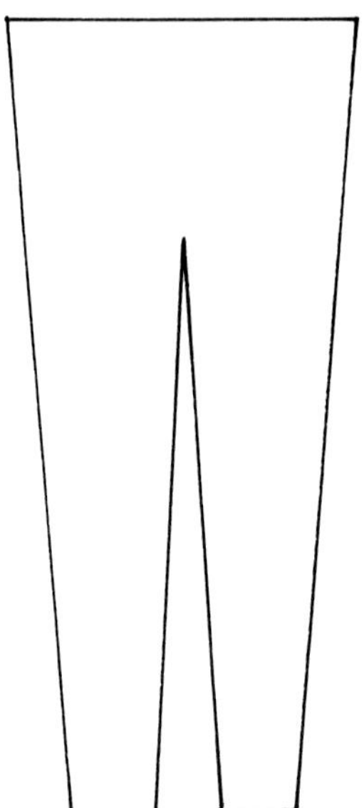

Hose reach from waist down.

Black shoes with swirling gold design. Black stockings. (Shoes were not made in "rights" and "lefts" until a much later date.)

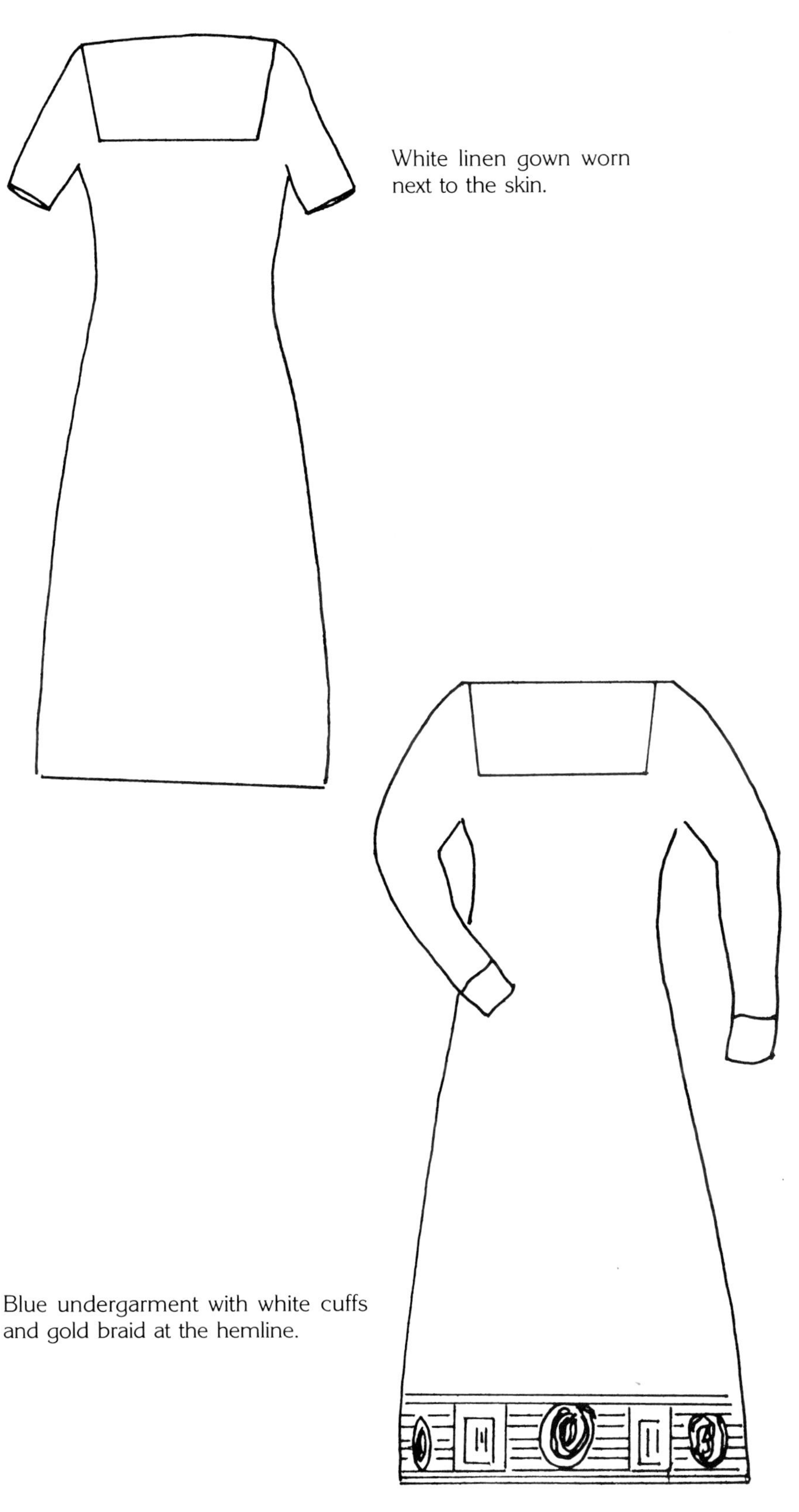

White linen gown worn
next to the skin.

Blue undergarment with white cuffs
and gold braid at the hemline.

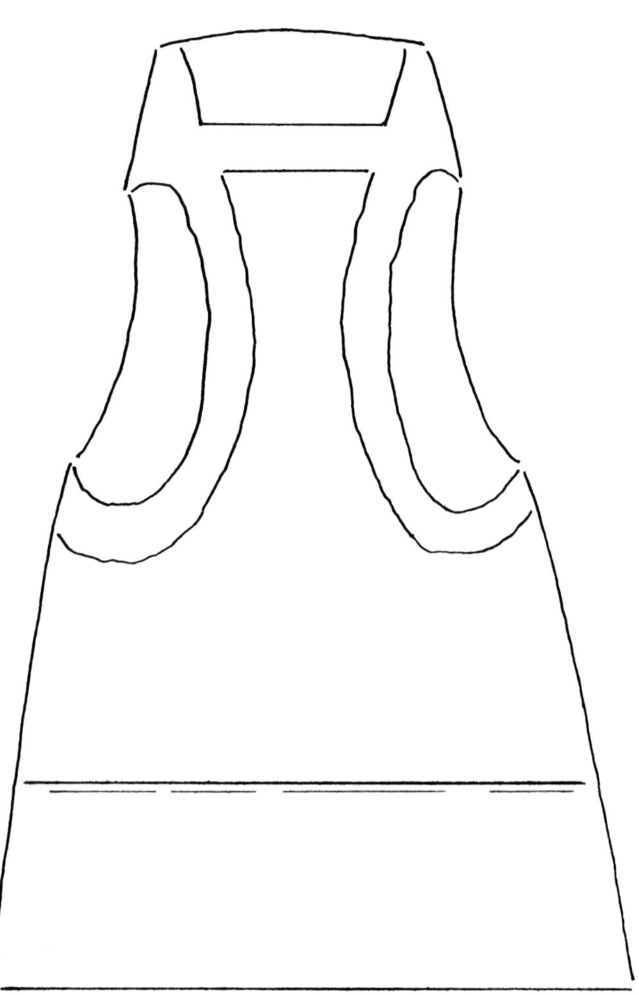

Specially shaped gold cloth gown with white velvet trimming and white satin lining.

Red slippers. White stockings. Gold garters.

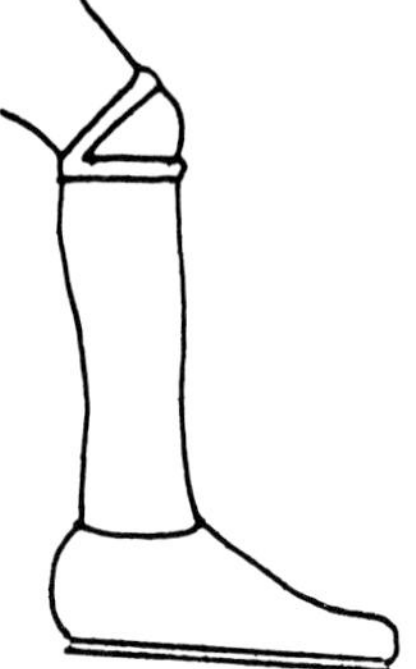

LADY MARY MARGARET

England, 1565

Lady Mary Margaret represents the continuing Elizabethan feudal custom of child marriage among the great families in 1565, mostly for one of three reasons.

For peace: To unite a strong political warring noble families.

        To unite two warring countries.

        To unite two warring religions.

For protection of the child and the family's property. Under feudal law, the Crown could take over a child's estates in the event of death of proper legal guardians and if she had no dowry, she would probably have to enter a convent.

For gain: To increase the parents' worth or repair their fortunes, as the marriage settlement was made when the contract was signed.

According to one of their marriage laws, "Woman hath divers special ages." At seven, her father may tax his tenants to provide a

daughter's dowry. Elizabethans believed that seven was the age of reason. At nine, she deserves to receive the dowry. At 12, capable of consent to marriage; at 14 ready for marriage and at 16, she is "Past the Lord's tender of a husband."

If the betrothal contract was made before seven, at the time of marriage, should the underage party dislike the future partner, the contract could be voided. If seven or over, the contract must be honored.

Twelve was the legal dividing line between child and woman. If the marriage was consummated at 12, she could not disagree afterward; if it was not consummated before 12, she might dissent until she was 14.

The grooms were often older than the brides. There was one little girl who was "married" and "widowed" three times before she was 11. She later became the Duchess of Devonshire.

A law regarding unmarried women inflicted rather harsh measures. "If a woman between the ages of twelve and forty be unmarried and out-of-work, she can be forced, by proper authorities, to serve by day, week or year in any work they think proper, at whatever wages they approve, under penalty of being committed to prison until she will work." This reflects the attitude of Elizabethan parents, rich and poor, who believed that "Children be taught some employment, that they may get their living with honesty and truth."

For consummation, it was the same as that of the Romans, 12 for girls and 14 for boys. The evils of early marriage and early childbearing were obvious to the Elizabethans and only on rare occasions was it permitted. Writing about this custom, Geoffrey Fenton said, "It is wrong to have more respect for the ability of the body than the capacity of the mind."

Parents desired to protect their children, especially their girls. A father chose his daughter's suitor and arranged her marriage. Her mother taught her to "Fear God, love virtue, hate vice and disdain idleness." Obedience was expected as a matter of course and good manners were stressed. Custom endorsed parental authority.

The first Queen Elizabeth, a paragon of learning herself and better educated than most great men of her time, helped popularize education for women. Cultured, intelligent girls became the ideal and such daughters were prized in Elizabethan families because they made better marriages. They believed "A well nurtured and mannerly maiden is a polished jewel of a palace and the honor of her father's house."

Costume

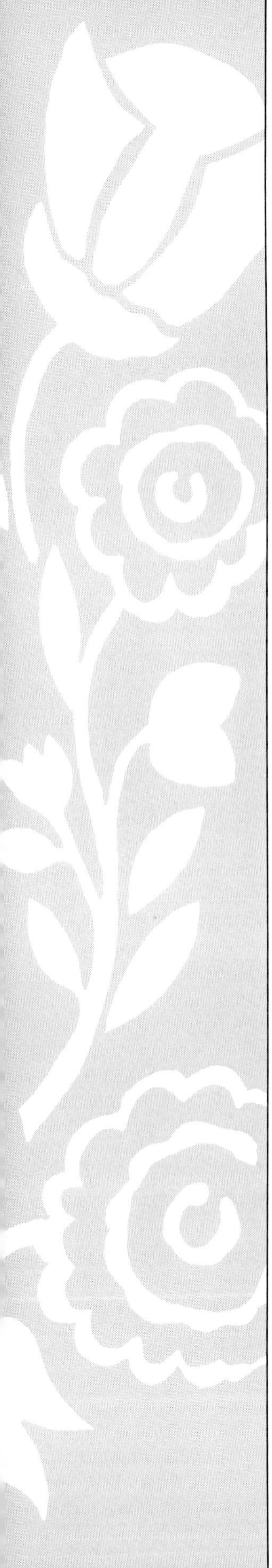

Lady Mary Margaret (we call her Little Bit) demonstrates the great chic of the miniature replicas of adult costumes in every way.

She wears the costume of the period; chartreuse green was very fashionable. Her outer robe is jeweled with pearls and opals, following the large stylized pattern of the fabric. Opals symbolized very good luck and were extremely popular at the time.

Her skirt is held out by the French farthingale's steel hoop. Her bodice is actually a corset lined with heavy linen. Steel or oak strips were slipped into vertical slots for boning. This stiff bodice-corset was introduced into England by 13-year-old Catherine of Aragon who married the Prince of Wales in 1533.

Little Bit wears the closed ruff of children and married women. Maidens wore the huge open ruff and deep decolletage like Elizabeth I, actually symbols of virginity, although it is difficult to believe for sometimes the entire bosom was exposed!

She had two elegant petticoats and a third, the knee-length linen shift, always worn next to the skin.

Stockings were now rolled above the knee and gartered there. Her shoes are the newest fashion, delicate colored velvet with cork soles and low heels.

Her hat is made from a piece of 16th century Italian velvet so she is wearing a fabric from the period she represents. These tiny little feather hats were a favorite place to display important jewels. The plainly dressed hair brought earrings back into fashion.

The greenery is a sprig of rosemary, symbolizing love and loyalty, a custom introduced into England by Anne of Cleves when she married Henry VIII. English brides liked the idea and adopted it, another instance of a royal marriage setting a wedding fashion.

Veils were seldom used. Noble brides wore caps and matching gloves; city brides — hats; country brides — garlands of fresh flowers and wheat. English women did not wear panties until the mid 18th century.

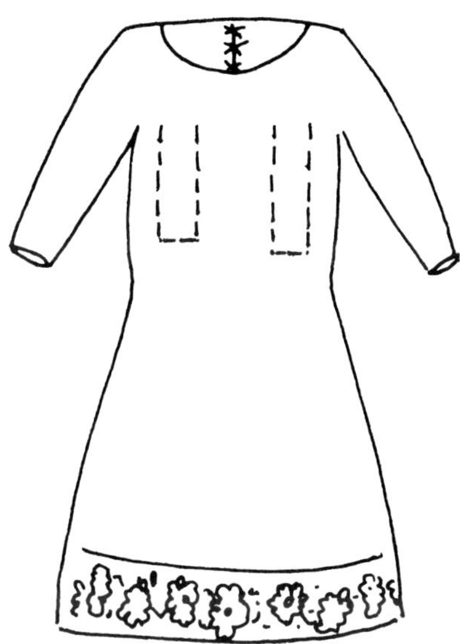

Silver cloth bodice with spaces for thin oak or steel braces. Embroidered flowers at the hemline. White silk lining.

Gold earrings.

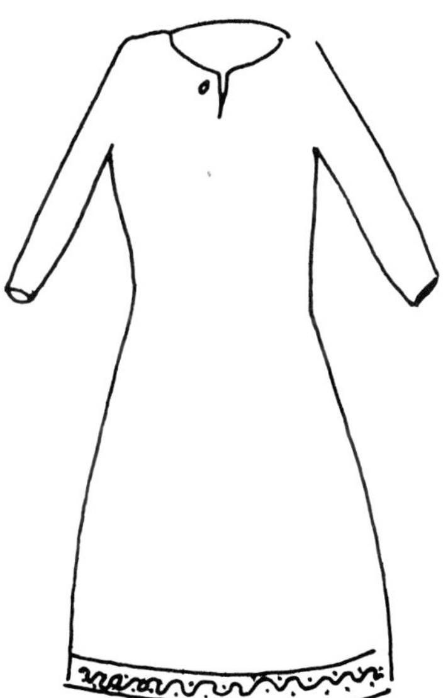

Second petticoat of tiny patterned white silk. Openwork silver lace at the hemline.

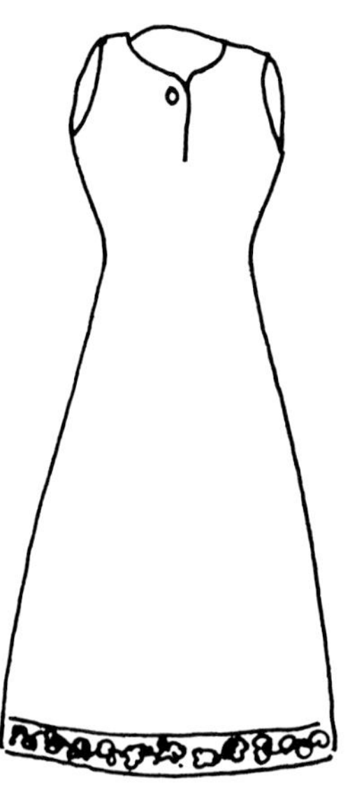

Third petticoat of white linen trimmed with pastel-colored flowers.

Green velvet hat with feather.

Pink velvet shoes with cork soles and low heels. Rolled white stockings with green garters worn above the knees.

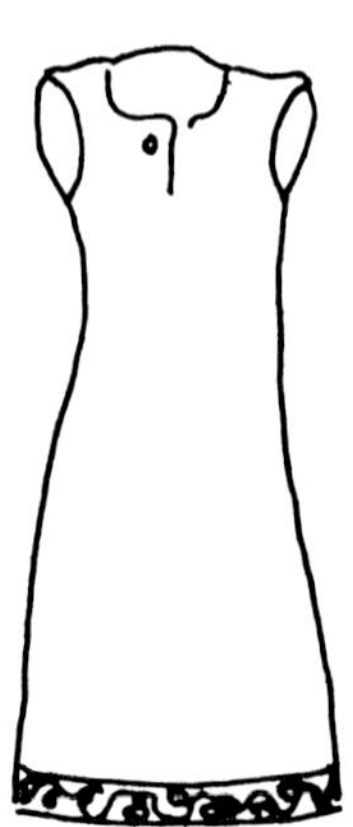

Knee-length linen with lace.

Customs

The wedding feast was held in the groom's home where he and the bride presented their friends with gifts of garters and gloves. This is probably the origin of the custom of modern grooms presenting their ushers with new gloves.

Wedding cakes were now small, rectangular and individual, about the size of petit fours and made like white fruit cake. The bride was greeted with a shower of these little cakes, thrown by the guests as she entered the banquet room; the cakes alighting on her head and shoulders was an especially good omen, relic of the ancient British custom of breaking the marriage cake over the bride's head as a fertility symbol.

MARIE LOUISE

France, 1720

Costume

Marie Louise illustrates the ancient custom of conducing the bride to bed or as it was more commonly called, "Bedding the Bride." This was in France in 1720.

She wears a handsome dressing gown, called a contouche in France and a sack-gown in England. Plain silks and satins in lighter colors were coming into style. However, the large floral patterns of the fashionable brocades were still in vogue and were carried over into embroidery, as shown by the large motifs trimming this robe.

The box pleats in the back give it fullness and it fastens down the front with gay ribbon bows. Sleeves are pleated vertically, the cuffs horizontally. The lining is finished with a lace band at the hemline. Under the dressing gown she wears an ivory silk nightgown trimmed with lace. Her nightcap matches the gown. She also has pink brocade mules with a ruching trim.

This charming style came from the theater. It was brought into fashion by the French actress Mme. Dancourt, who first wore it on the Parisian stage in 1703 when she was playing a part where she was supposed to be pregnant. The voluminous folds in the back detracts from the front fullness and she evidently wanted a costume that would be becoming and attractive on stage. It was so successful, she called the gown her "Andrienne" for the name of the comedy in which she was playing.

Fashionable women adopted it at once. It was a welcome change from the stiff bodices, hoops and heavy petticoats they had been wearing. It went through a number of changes and adaptations, rapidly graduating from the boudoir to a comfortable, easy informal dress worn indoors and later, for formal occasions. The best known of the formal style is that with the so-called "Watteau pleats" — two big box pleats in the back. Some even thought Watteau invented the style but it was called "Watteau" only because he painted so many charming examples of it.

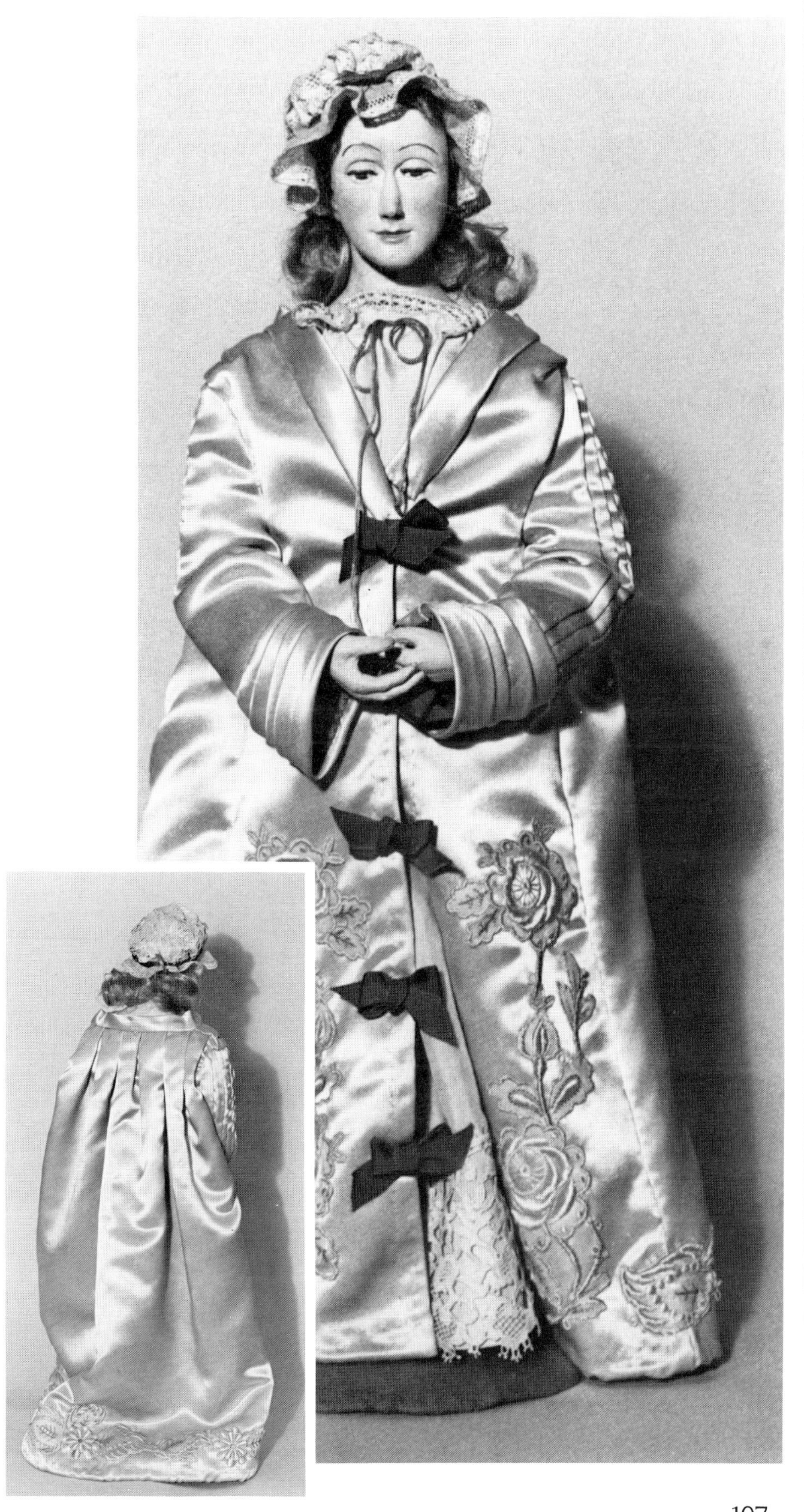

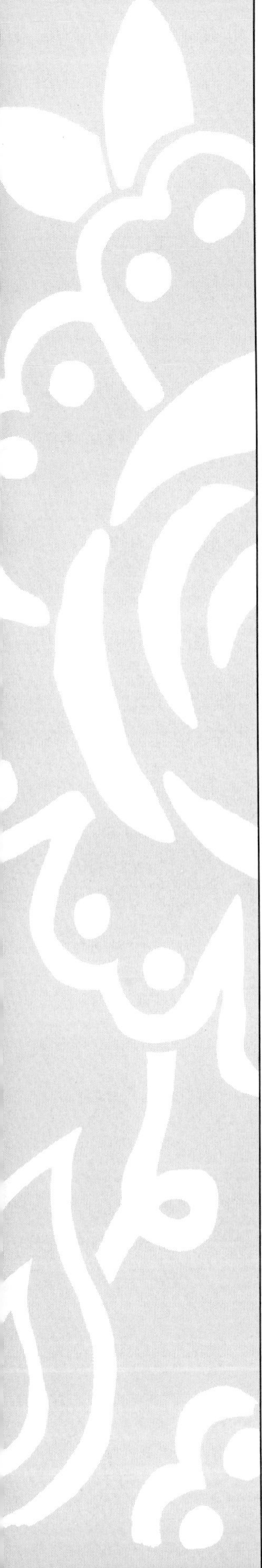

Hair was worn shoulder length, as the neat coiffure was popular. However, a bride still wore it flowing, intimating virginity.

Customs

The ancient custom of bedding the bride goes back to Old Testament times when the bridal procession led directly to the bridal tent where the marriage was promptly, almost publicly, consummated.

Witnessing the consummation was a ritual of great age and almost universal extent, as much a part of a wedding as the exchange of rings and the recital of vows. A wedding was a moment to rejoice at the eternal renewal of life that was promised by the union of a man and a woman. It was this last purpose that generally determined the special elements of wedding celebrations.

Requiring witnesses to the bridal bedding may have come from the early Teutonic tribes who considered a marriage valid only if it could be proven that the bride and groom had been together under the same blanket.

The Greeks and Romans led the bridal couple to the nuptial chamber and waited outside the closed door until the groom announced that the marriage had been consummated.

In the Middle Ages the bridal chamber was considered almost sacred ground. Dressed for bed, the couple knelt while the priest blessed the nuptial couch. The bed would often be strewn with roses and censed, like an altar. Sometimes the newly married pair would abstain from consummation the first night, or even the first three nights, in honor of the Virgin Mary, to whom they prayed until they fell asleep.

Less devout couples were sometimes forced to wait until midnight before the priest would pronounce a benediction, unless handsomely paid for it. They dared not do without this blessing in fear of excommunication.

Being escorted to the bridal bed in the presence of witnesses was prescribed by Church Law, but that was not until the mid 16th century. Their wedding rings were the only legal records of the marriage as there were no wedding certificates as we know today.

The family was the basic social unit in Europe and the British Isles for more than 1000 years, from the fall of the Roman Empire to the discovery of the New World. Within this familial society, a

Dressing gown with applied band of lace
at neck, sleeves and bottom.

Lace nightcap.

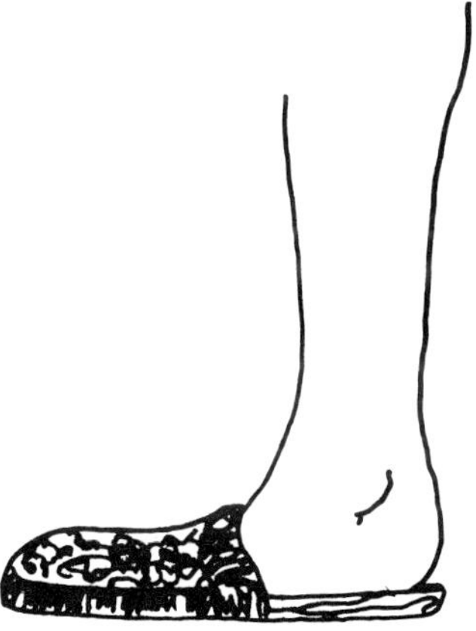

Brocade mules with ruching trim.

wedding was a highly important event, especially for royalty and the nobility.

So it was according to customary usage and polite sentiment that the domestic celebration of a marriage was concluded with a reception of the guests in the bridal chamber, with the bridal couple seated in bed.

We must remember that the beds were quite large and heavily curtained so that there was a degree of privacy.

In the 17th and 18th centuries in Europe and in Britain bedding the bride was always observed, attended by many superstitions and ceremonies.

After the evening's feasting and dancing were concluded, the bridesmaids conducted the bride to the bridal bedroom where they undressed her, making sure to take away all pins, to guard against bad luck, also untying all knots, ensuring her an easy childbirth.

Wearing a handsome dressing gown over her night robe, they seated her in bed and warned her to be sure not to lose her nightcap, to hold onto it with both hands for if she lost it, that would be very bad luck!

Meanwhile, the groomsmen were preparing the groom. When he was ready, he was escorted to the bride's room, also wearing an elegant dressing gown and nightcap. There he joined the bride in bed.

The guests then entered to drink to their health, wish them joy, sing rowdy wedding songs and in England, see the bridal party "fling the stocking."

The bridesmaids sat on the bride's side of the great bed, holding her stockings, the groomsmen on the other side holding his, all with their backs to the bridal couple. At a given signal, they flung the stockings over their heads and if a girl could hit the groom with one, or a man the bride, it was a sign that the thrower would soon be married.

After this, the priest blessed the bed. Following the blessing, the couple was served the Benediction Posset in a handsome silver cup. Made of wine, milk, eggs, sugar and spices, it was supposedly a mild aphrodisiac. "Wine will make a man lusty, and sugar will make him kind" was an ancient belief, particularly in England, where the wine used was sack and because of it, the drink was called a sack posset. (Sack is a form of sherry.)

Today bridesmaids help the bride change her clothes for the honeymoon trip and the best man assists the groom.

English and French royalty observed these customs for centuries. In 1747 the Dauphin of France, Louis XV's son, married Marie Josephe of Saxony. Only 18, the Dauphin was a shy, retiring young man. Seated stiffly on his wedding bed with his bride beside him, he received the horde of curious courtiers. His ancestors had been doing this on their wedding nights for years; however, this did not make it any easier for young Louis. He took one look at that glittering crowd and disappeared under the bedclothes, to the consternation of the guests — but not his bride, who was quite composed and obviously enjoyed herself, without the help of her groom.

Charles I of England was the first British monarch to flout custom. He led the party to the entrance of the nuptial chamber, then slammed the door and locked it in their faces. He and his bride than retired to the bridal bed unwitnessed which was considered quite scandalous.

Most royal and noble couples put up with the ceremony until the early 19th century.

Privacy in the bedroom is a comparatively modern refinement. In previous times, the apartments used for repose at night were used for the reception of visitors by day. Frequently, high ranking men and women received friends, visitors and tradesmen in dressing gowns.

Many societies, including our own, have not considered a marriage valid, no matter how elaborate the wedding ceremony, unless consummated. This was especially important at royal weddings where the consummation of the marriage was usually also the consummation of an important alliance.

When Mary Stuart married the Prince of Orange, they observed blessing the bed, stocking throwing and Benediction Posset. Her father, Charles I, himself drew the curtains around their bed after they emptied the posset cup.

George III and Queen Charlotte were the first royal British couple whose wedding celebrations in 1721 dispensed with the stocking throwing and Benediction Posset, by premarital arrangements for the wedding.

Here is an old bridal-bed benediction from Brittany (1875): "Lord bless the bed and those you find there; bless these dear children, as you have blessed Toby and Sara; deign to bless them also Lord, to the end, that in your name, they will live and grow old and multiply by Christ our Lord. Thus be it. Amen."

SELECTED BIBLIOGRAPHY

Bernstein. *Masterpieces of Women's Costumes of the 18th and 19th Centuries.* N.Y.: Crown Publishers, Inc., 1959.

Brooke & Laver. *English Costume of the 14th Through the 19th Century.* N.Y.: Macmillan Publishing Co., 1937.

Calthrop, Dion. *English Costume, Volume III.* London, England: Adam & Charles Black, Ltd., 1906.

Crawford, M.D.C. *Heritage of Cotton.* N.Y.: Grossett & Dunlap, Inc., 1924.

Davenport, Milia. *The Book of Costume.* N.Y.: Crown Publishers, Inc., 1948.

Evans, Mary. *Costume Throughout the Ages.* Philadelphia, PA.: J. B. Lippincott Co., 1930.

Hughes, Therle. *English Domestic Needlework.* N.Y.: Macmillan Publishing Co., 1961.

Lepage-Medvey. *French Costumes.* Westport, Conn.: Hyperion Press, 1939.

Morse, H. K. *Elizabethan Pageantry.* London, England: Studio, 1934.

Norris, Herbert. *Costume & Fashion, Volume III, Book 2.* N.Y.: E.P. Dutton & Co., 1938.

von Boehn, Max. *Modes & Manners, Volume III.* Philadelphia, PA.: J. B. Lippincott Co., 1932.

Wilcox, R. Turner. *The Mode in Footwear.* N.Y.: Charles Scribner's Sons, 1948.

------. *The Mode in Hats and Head-dresses.* N.Y.: Charles Scribner's Sons, 1952.